Roads to Addiction
Highways to Recovery

The Brian Masters Story

Introduction

This is the true story of a prosperous man and the life changing contributors leading to an addictive disease; in his case, alcohol. Brian Masters endured a contentious divorce, a traumatic attack on his life, betrayal, financial ruin, abandonment, and constant emotional and physical pain, due to a chronic infection resulting from a series of medical mistakes. Alcohol helped him cope, until alcoholism became the real problem.

Follow Brian through hospitals, rehabs, shelters, the streets, the people, and the unique subculture of the homeless and/or afflicted. The story is told through Brian's personal narrative and excerpts from his journals, augmented by medical records, shelter records, and police reports. As the story unfolds, Brian discovers multiple paths leading to recovery, providing you with an emotionally uplifting reality of hope for people.

This is Brian Masters' story, but he invites the reader to imagine what it was like: to endure chronic pain, to trust no one, to live solely by your wits, to get down and dirty for the sake of survival. Brian Masters could be any one of us, and he asks simply, "Walk in my shoes." It may help save your own life or the life of a loved one.

Paths to Addiction – Highways to Recovery: The Brian Masters Story

Brian Masters

www.addictionrealityeducation.com

First edition Brian Masters 2017: ASIN: B078J9PYW1

ISBN 9781976809705

Dedication

Roads to Addiction – Highways to Recovery is dedicated to all the men, women, and young adults who seriously attempt all the Beach Head Action Plans to normalcy and consistently increase the scores on the Recovery Capital Scale.

They deserve the respect for working and succeeding, no matter how many times they attempt the multiple paths.

Table of Contents

Preface

What This Book Is

The intention of this book is to share my real-life experiences to help young people and adults understand the plight of the homeless, the addicted, or the financially destitute. This book is my attempt to have you touch the pain and sadness that people endure. It is will also provide you with an emotionally uplifting reality of hope for people; those who succeed and those who do not. Should any person's life be saved, or path be changed by this book, then what I have seen and experienced was worth it.

All the places, people, and events in this book are real. I've changed the names of the people to protect their privacy.

To start you off, read these comments made by three of the people I came to know during my time on the streets. How would **you** have answered?

> When my grandma asked me what I wanted to be in life, I DID NOT answer, "I want to be a woman who has not had a bath in a week, gave a blow job this morning so I could stick a needle in my arm later today."
>
> When asked by my college professor, what will you do with all that education? I DID NOT ANSWER: "I will find a good spot, near some trees, next to the hair styling shop off main street and below the church where no one can see me. I will dig a hole for my vodka bottles where no one can find them and steal them."
>
> When asked by my roommate, what's up for the weekend? I ANSWERED: "I am taking the bus to Framingham. Head over to Main and Rt. 126, where Need It Now girls hang out and

pleasure one of them for $30; hopefully $50 if I should find it.

One had developed Wernicke-Korsakoff Syndrome--street name is Wet Brain. One was a prostitute from my shelter. One was a roommate in a shelter, who later threatened to kill me because I knew too much.

During the nor'easters (heavy storms off the Atlantic Ocean) of 2015, I shuffled through the snow and ice in towns just outside Boston, Massachusetts to get to the library to send out resumes and be warm. I often said, "No one would believe what I have been through." Or I would say, "Someone needs to let people know what is going on out here, before it happens to them."

This book is an attempt to follow through on those thoughts. I want people to recognize what is really happening. The disease of addiction, whether it is genetic, environmental, or a combination of both, is a path of self-destruction and death. And worst of all it creates innocent victims of the babies and children born to addicts. I want people to be educated before they take their first snort, pop their first pill, shoot their first injection, or drink their first glass. Once armed with the facts and exposed to the realities of the path that could await them, it now becomes a choice--do you want this disease? Do you want to be a person who says something like the quotes above?

What This Book is Not

This book is not a complete answer to the problem of addiction. If you watch TV, you will see ads about "Addiction." How the spokesperson or CEO was once an addict but was cured--cured *because of their program*. When I was at a few evaluation centers and the TV aired those commercials, everyone would laugh, especially the young adults. I would wonder, why are these people laughing? Then it hit me. As addicts, we are taught that there is no cure. This commercial and others like it were a joke. The people who were being held in an evaluation center for substance use and mental issues saw no hope. So, I say, what I share in this book is not a cure.

The material in this book is not a high-level analysis of psychology, genetics, or the environment.

What's in this book is not an argument for what works and what does not work.

I'm not attempting to scare you away from controlled and non-controlled substances.

I'm not suggesting that any one methodology of sobriety is correct or the best; though I do discourage Recoveryism in any form.

And by any means, I don't think that an addict is a bad person tortured by the lack of the "right stuff." I fully agree with comments made by Alva Noe, in her discussion of the book "Unbroken Brain," by Maia Szalavitz.

> Addicts, so the moralist say, are people who won't say no. They consume beyond restraint and recklessly indulge their pleasures. This is a bad way to live. Addicts are bad. The moralist gets something right, I believe. The moralist is right, for example, that the addict's life is seriously and even morally messed up. Addicts are closed and shut down. This is bad. This is a bad and painful and sad way to be. But the moralist is wrong to think this is somehow a moral failing of the addict. Addicts are not bad.

This book is an attempt to offer a perspective of hope. By understanding the realities that can await you, I hope you will identify with the people, events, organizations, and circumstances I describe. Then you can take the actions necessary to prevent this future or turn it around now.

What I Hope You Will Learn from this Book

Your perception of my travels, the people I have met, and the choices I made will be totally up to you; your judgement might be entirely different. Yet, by laying out the events I experienced, I can provide insight, which may influence your decision to keep full control of legal substances and stay away from controlled substances. I hope that after reading this book, you will be educated enough to say, "I remember that event or episode from Brian's book! It stops now!"

I cannot stress strongly enough what you will go through mentally and physically if you take the path I was on. I can tell you of my experience, what I have seen, and the interpretation of people I met. Yet, I realize different experiences bring different perspectives.

The Meaning of Italics and Blocks of Text to the Reader

Italics

My use of Italics is to explain the event and what I think the reader may want to absorb. It allows me to talk to you as if I were sitting across from you at a table.

Italics will be used to express what was is in my mind or heart at the time. I want to express something in my own words about the reality you are reading about.

Blocked Text

Text indented on the left and right indicates an event or situation that has special meaning. The text is indented from the rest of the narrative so that you can have a more specific understanding of the environment and/or the character of a person. This means there is no smooth thread that ties one event to another other than the time line of what I lived through. This allows me to focus on an event without building a lengthy story around the episode.

The Challenge

Walk in My Shoes

One of the hardest things to do in life is to walk in someone else's shoes. Yet, to help understand the reality of what someone is experiencing, you must try to do just that. By creating a bond, you are in a good position to feel what someone feels, which leads to understanding an action, or even better, helps you judge the person with compassion.

The people I have met and continue to meet have their own stories. So, as we move through this book, I will elaborate on people's background. The challenge for you, as the reader, is to "walk in my shoes."

Strip Away Preconceived Conceptions

Throughout this book you will meet people:

•	Who had been homeless and addicted and who have regained their footing

•	Who understand the circumstances because of how they were raised

•	Who had close family and friends who have suffered

•	Who were executives and/or engineers prior to masking their addiction

- Who have a career or job that involves providing the care addicts require

- Who want to let others know that they are and never will be as low as "those" people are

- Who have a caring personality

Pride is not an option when suffering from homelessness, depression, addiction, and a lack of self-worth. As the reader, you must strip away the prejudice you have toward the people you meet. You cannot walk in their shoes if you won't--that is the challenge.

You may think that these challenges are easy and just common sense. It is my challenge to make sure you see why they are not. There was a man who was hiding his vodka bottles. When I came through the bushes, and we saw each other face to face, he was scared stiff. Not that I would turn him in or spit at him. His eyes bulged in fear because I knew where he hid his stash. "Trust no one and suspect everyone."

Phase 1--
The Home-The Contributors-The Road-The Streets

Smile – All is Well – Or is It?

I feel you need to know about me, Brian Masters, the author. The events I describe here led to drinking, loneliness, depression, anxiety, and feelings of desperation. Through positive events, good people, educators, and my belief in a higher power, what seemed to be hopeless changed for the better. I would like to make it clear to you that I know different people have different life experiences. I am sharing my background and story, so you can understand or identify with what I describe. Please create your own "mile high view" as we travel through the book. Let's work together and prevent you and others from taking the wrong path.

I had no clue that 2007 would be the year that started a series of circumstances that would change my life. The interesting fact is that if these events had not happened, a whole new world of learning would have never come to me. My life was severely affected; yet, I know, along the way, others were positively impacted by me being here.

Mile High View of Brian Masters

Success and a satisfying new direction: In December 2006, I received my Black Belt in Kenpo Karate. Though I had been studying various styles of martial arts since I was fifteen years-old, this achievement was substantial. For a man my age, I was proud that I had held my own compared to men twenty years younger than me. In the eyes of most karate practitioners in the United States, I was a confirmed teacher and had earned the respect of my peers. This reinforced my desire to stay in the best shape I could and enjoy teaching the art to people age 13 and up, for as long as I was able.

My years as a software salesperson were winding down but I was still on the leading edge of analytic technology, making a six-figure income consistently. My network of peers and executives was well established, so crossing over to another job was easier than it is for most at my age. In other words, for the time being, I felt secure for the future.

It was at this point I decided to act on a retirement plan that would make me happy. My wife, who was in the travel industry, had inadvertently put a goal in my mind. Because she was selling travel, I was able to visit cruise ships as they came to Boston Harbor. Travel people would be wined and dined so they would recommend the company and the ships. During a tour, it was apparent that some of the ship lines, which catered to the over-forty crowd, had no classes in self-protection and safety awareness. It was then my goal for retirement was born. I wanted to offer over-forty cruise ship passengers effective, satisfying, and not overly stressful self-defense classes. At the same time, I could travel to different ports of call while enjoying an art I knew well.

I surveyed six cruise lines and only one had such an offering. I designed a proposal and approached three cruise lines with my business plan. At the same time, I made an agreement with my instructor, Master Henry Agri, that I could use the school's name once I received my third-degree black belt. Two out of three companies were interested. How could this plan go wrong for a clean cut, blue eyed man, in great shape, who could teach?

Within two years, my son would be out of the university and he would have no debt. My yearly income goals would hold all investments stable and allow for more, less risky, investments. The stock markets were at their highest levels, each 13,700 points/2500 points in the NYSE and NASDAQ respectively. Any improvement in the market meant more liquid assets would be added to my existing net 1.35-million-dollar estate. Our primary house would be paid for in four years and our lake house would be paid for in nine years. My wife and I could decide on next steps, and all would be good.

At this point, I was in control of my social drinking, but the drinking increased during down periods. This was depression, masking the feeling of old age; worst of all was that there was no one to check my behavior. My primary doctor issued standard anti-depressants, and I felt better.

The marital bombshell: Then came March of 2007. After a St. Patrick's Day reunion in my home town of Syracuse, my friends, Mike Garrison, Tom Garrison, and I drove back to our current homes in Massachusetts. Our return to Upstate New York was an annual event that allowed us to see high school and college friends and let loose. The guys picked up their cars at my home. Tom went his way to Chelmsford, Mike to Canton, and I stayed at my raised ranch in Westborough.

On the evening of March 19th, my wife Linda asked if we could have a glass of wine out by the pool or the indoor porch. I quickly closed my Laptop and study room door, went down to the downstairs game room, and made us drinks. As I sat down there was, only what I can describe as, a cold neutral zone between us. Out of nowhere, Linda said, "I do not love you, I don't want to be with you, I do not want to make love to you, I don't want to have sex with you, and I do not want you spending any more of my money!"

This was the furthest thing from my mind; to say I was shocked is an understatement. These comments were the last words I had anticipated to hear from her. I was mentally and physically stunned, and nothing can express my feelings. I was in a fog. All the normal questions came to mind: "Why me? What did I do?" In twenty-three years, I had not had another woman other than a kiss; I must have missed something. I wasn't the greatest lover in the world, but I wasn't bad either. Our relationship never had any type of physical or mental abuse. We seemed to be happy.

A common statement is that "It takes two to tango!" Well, it must have been that time in life for Brian and Linda, and there was no stopping it. Right or wrong, I dug in my heels for a fight.

The Contributors to Ground Zero

Any life changing event can be a contributor to substance use. The event, whether big or small, is only relevant to the person affected. Fighting in a war, losing a job, and catching a partner cheating are some examples. So, think of an event or events that you or a friend may have had or are experiencing. Five significant life-altering changes started my downward journey in motion. These events are not an excuse, but they were all contributors.

Divorce

Our version of the War of the Roses had begun: At the official signing of the divorce papers, the lawyers on both sides said it was the worse divorce case they had seen in Worcester County, other than a divorce that involved children under the age of eighteen.

People say, never get divorced because you will lose all your money. Neena Shots, my attorney, stopped me one day as I was leaving her office. She said, "at the end of it all, you will be broke!" I just smiled and closed the door, thinking to myself, "Not me!"

Yes, money will be lost, but it's the mental stress that eats your rational thinking alive. That is why you will hear only divorce conversation from people who are going through a divorce. One way to mask the reality of it all was alcohol and drugs.

Each month, communication eroded more and more. Linda's world of friends and my world of friends became entirely different. Fortunately, *for my future*, I kept past relationships in place. Linda took a sales position in Worcester and hung with people who lived in that area.

By the time September 2007 came, divorce papers were filed, restraining orders were in place, and court dates were set. I was left without a home or a base of operations. The daily onslaught of requests from her attorney never stopped. My ability to hold a job, let alone get another was becoming impossible. I began to drink to reduce tremors and anxiety. I accompanied this with the comfort of new women (now that I was free) and hanging out with men friends who enabled the desire to drink.

At this stage, people will tell you not to party with your favorite substance. I know my investment broker and karate instructor told me that, but I did not listen! There was more stress release from the real world with friends who drank. I should have stuck to health and business--that is my advice to you if you are at this stage of any life changing event.

A crash course in divorce finance: Once divorce papers are filed, the law requires that there is a lockdown on the joint estate. This includes money, houses, furniture, cars, and bank accounts. Everything the two of you have built. To release either party from any part of the estate, both parties need to agree. From the estate, both parties are allowed money to live and pay bills until the terms of the divorce are finalized. So, from the cash and assets you have, attorney fees, living expenses, all bills associated to keep the estate going, tuition, and other items are released (subtracted) from the estate bucket. The lawyers and courts have control. You literally watch what you worked so hard to attain deteriorate.

In my case, the court had made me immediately homeless. My residence at the lake had been divided between my wife and me, so living at the lake full time was not an option. This was a foreshadow of what was to come.

Friends: The times I felt most at ease was with close friends, especially when things got tough. The people I loved, at that point, were the ones who came to my aid.

There was Tom Garrison and his wife Ester. Both were retired and had a house on Martha's Vineyard and an elegant home in Chelmsford, MA. Tom Garrison allowed me to stay two weeks while I was organizing my files for the divorce. Jeff Lent was a friend I had become close to through business, house parties, and lunches. While he was vacationing in France for two weeks, he let me use his place. My woman friend, Jennifer, had separated from her husband Peter. Since Peter was barred from their home, I could have their office for divorce paperwork and the job search. Other friends provided moral support and housing when possible.

The single most dangerous choice we can make, no matter what the circumstances, is to seek out friends who are equally miserable as you. They will come out of the woodwork, and unfortunately, they will reinforce substance use.

Trauma

The assault on my life: Linda and I had gone our separate ways regarding friends and activities since March of 2007. Both of us had our own foundations which very rarely touched each other's lives. I had befriended couples from different towns. These couples were also having marital or partner problems, which started the "misery likes company" parties.

On November 26th, 2007, the night before Thanksgiving Day, five of my friends and I were having drinks at the local VFW, the only bar open at that time of night. The front door burst open and without warning, a man rushed twenty feet at a full gallop and struck me on the right side of my head, one inch from my temple. In other words, I was "cold cocked," knocked out, and hit the floor. Nothing was stopping Randy Landers from pounding my head and kicking my body. Fortunately, the ladies I was with pulled him from me only to have Randy attack them before running out the door. It is interesting to note that the only other man in our group, Larry, had run for the bathroom and stayed there until the police arrived.

I was taken to the hospital, treated for cuts, a concussion, and released. Pain was replaced by shock, which was replaced by depression and the question, "Why?"

Physical damage done: My lower teeth punctured my lower lip. My dentist of 15 years, told me my jaw was out of place and might remain that way. The severe beating, I took became apparent from the photograph of bruises extending from my head to my thighs. My friend Jennifer, who witnessed the beating, bought a camera and took pictures after I returned to the hospital. One day while talking to my neighbor, Billy LaDuc, at a local townie sports bar, I watched his mouth moving and I could hear nothing. All the conversations behind me were blocking sound in front of me. After hearing tests by Dr. Ladders, I learned that the pitches had changed from the test the year before; my hearing on the right side had diminished. The eye tests on the right eye had a similar result.

The physical tremors started to show a month later. The most shocking effect of the attack was my inability to spar in martial arts. When I stepped out to fight at the karate school or tournament, I froze like a popsicle. I had no control of my body movements.

Then the mental effect of the attack became apparent. Fear and anxiety were a constant emotion. If anyone approached or touched me on the right side, I raised my arm to block and my fist to fight. These actions were 100 percent involuntary and unstoppable. I recognized this type of behavior from the men I knew who come back to our dojo after serving in combat, and from documentaries about vets coming back from the Middle East. I speculated that I had a form of post-traumatic stress disorder (PTSD).

Fighting two fronts: Shortly after Thanksgiving week ended, Landers was arrested for "assault with a shod foot." In other words, attempt to murder with a dangerous weapon, *his feet*. This charge is a felony in Massachusetts. Why, is kicking a person with a foot a felony? Because, in the past, men or women would wear shoes with a pointed tip. They would use the sharp tip as a weapon to either attack or defend themselves. Since people had died from the shoe attacks, it became a crime to kick a person while wearing a shoe.

Now, I was involved with two court cases: a civil probate case and a criminal case, both within the same county. There was nowhere I could go that somebody did not know about either one of the cases and would express their opinion. I could not escape the stress.

It is amazing how a small town reacts to personal drama. One day, while driving down Main Street, I saw the wife of a DPW worker I knew. She threw the middle finger gesture at me. Most know it as the "bird".

The drama is revealed: Why would Randy attack me, in a public place, in front of his wife Patricia Landers, Larry (a carpenter in town), Mary Hamill (a school teacher), Steve Fritz (a bartender), and Jennifer (my soon to be girlfriend)? During Randy's criminal case, my old medical records were entered into court to show *that I had perjured myself*. The judge told me *to stand, not be sworn in, and listen*. Randy's lawyer stated to the judge that evidence was provided by Mrs. Masters and would show that the medical conditions I attributed, under oath, to the attack were actually pre-existing. Immediately, everyone realized that there was some relationship between Randy and my soon to be ex-wife. This was a serious attempt to put me in jail! It was my luck that the Judge, knowing of the divorce, saw through the attempt by both people and his lawyer; the Judge threw out the motion.

Though the legal attempt failed, the link between Linda Masters and Randy Landers was established. Poor Randy Landers--he was a well-known, wealthy alcoholic who was told that I was sleeping with his wife. The truth surprised everyone. Larry, the man who had hid in the bathroom during the attack, was the man who was involved with Randy's wife, Patricia. Randy was fed the wrong information. One other important piece of information is that if I died during the divorce, the estate would be $500,000 richer from the life insurance, for a total of two million dollars. The only beneficiary

14

would be Linda Masters. Also, if I were arrested and jailed at any time during an active divorce, according to Massachusetts law, the fifty-fifty rule of division of assets might not apply; I could lose my right to the assets in the estate.

Interesting, isn't it? This is material that would make a "tell all" novel or television show. What I want you to understand is that these events helped create a pattern of behavior that was not healthy for me. I needed to realize it was time to get serious help before allowing alcohol and depression to build to a critical level. In the medical field, depression is one of the top five sicknesses to address. The hospital therapists pushed my symptoms off to stress and alcohol. According to UMass records from my Primary Care Physician, Dr. Ford, I was diagnosis with "Situational Anxiety." I am sure that if I had been educated or seriously advised about the possibility of my condition, I would have acted. What I want you to understand is that you should not lie to yourself about alcohol or drug intake! Do not lie to yourself about your depression, fear, or anxiety. Take control as soon as you can--if you can. Considering the technology, we have at our finger tips, there should be no reason not to be informed to some extent.

2008 – The Great Recession:

Job loss and equity decline: The divorce was final by 2008. The devastated estate was divided equally. It was time to pick up the what was left and attempt to build a secure life. In my mind, security for my son and a place to call home were more important. Buying back the house that my son, Johnny, grew up in would create consistency in his life. His friends from school were close by, and activities would ease the traumatic changes. Johnny would have his old home in the summer of 2008. That was the plan anyway.

The new analytical predictive modeling software sale job I took showed great promise for the next five years. With my abilities to start up new businesses and my existing network, a solid six figure income would continue to be a strong possibility.

With a new president, hopes were high throughout the United States, except for the banking system. The instability and fraudulent use of capital crushed the economy into a second depression. What did this mean to me? The house was now worth half its value, money for new software in corporations dried up, and sales were nonexistent. The company that had employed me closed its doors and the job was gone. The math was simple and obvious. No money coming in and money going out led to taking funds from my 401 accounts. The 401, the house, and some cash were the last vestiges of twenty-five years of work.

I need to note that I was not alone in this disaster. Many of my friends could not sustain their houses or lifestyles during this time. You may have been one of them. But in my mind, success was always right around the corner. My patterns of dating women and meeting friends out for drinks and dinner did not change. Healthy choices were ignored. I didn't take the time to focus on my financial, emotional and spiritual needs and gain the support of true friends.

This was another point in time that healthier decisions could have been made.

For me, the changes in my life had taken a toll. The tremors were enhanced by the alcohol that was meant to stop them. Shaking was uncontrollable. Working out and teaching became inconsistent. Hangovers were part of the week. This led to my eyes being glazed and tired. These were the first behavioral and physical flags telling me to make new decisions.

Emotional devastation

The loss of my son's love: In early August 2007, Linda and I were fighting when our son Johnny blurted, "Why don't you two get a divorce!" I was the child of a divorce, so that was the last emotional burden I wanted to inflict on Johnny; but it was inevitable. Divorces are just fact. One evening in late September 2007, I rushed out to the house because I was late for karate, and I had left my home office computer on. Linda took the opportunity to open my email and found a note between Jennifer and me, which was suggestive, nothing more. But the note was enough to imply that there was a relationship. When I returned home, Linda physically beat me. This had happened before but only when she was under the influence. When I look back, I see it was an attempt to have me lose my temper and physically create a bruise on her body, but it did not work. In my mind, a man who beats a woman is scum. Unfortunately, my calling the police was a mistake because I was the man, and the man is the one to leave the premises.

After this event, Linda drove directly to Johnny's university and gave him the email material and told him stories. I was repeatedly advised by my attorney and friends to "take the high road!" They told me to not to go to the university and keep him out of the divorce in an attempt to put things straight. Well, that high road meant not pleading my position, and that meant Johnny came to dislike me as shown by his texted messages. By Christmas of 2007, there was no communication from him. I thought I had lost my son.

Fortunately for me, Johnny did come back to the house on extended school vacations, which was the very reason I had bought back the home. The time Johnny and I spent together during these vacations helped mend some of the damage done by the divorce; but what was done, was done.

Loneliness of 2010: By 2010, it was apparent that the so-called torrid love affair between Jennifer and me was nothing more than two people sharing the same problems. If time is a test, the relationship failed. But a house with one person can be unbearable, so internet dating became a play toy.

When Johnny was home, he taught me about the sites the kids used to expand their sexual possibilities. I was not going to argue with his generation's internet skills. Because of his tutoring, I met Sherry from two towns over. Sherry was 5'4", had black hair and was attractive. After a few months of occasional dating, getting together was an emotional drinking overdose. It turned out, Sherry was a closet alcoholic. The fact that she had a mastectomy and needed moral support fed right into my character flaw. I helped Sherry recover. I looked at it as a friend relationship, and that is the way it was, but the amount of drinking increased. One morning, I could not hold down water; I had to be near the bathroom to vomit. I got so bad that Sherry introduced me to AA. I admitted I was an alcoholic. Again, I missed the sign posts.

This is important to know! One of AA's and SMART's unwritten rules is to abstain from sexual relationships during recovery. The purpose of this rule is to allow you to focus on yourself and not be torn in different directions. Whether your problem is alcohol, cocaine, crack, opiate pills, heroin or all the above, the introduction of a partner will sidetrack your recovery efforts. Your partner's need may fog your determination to correct your own behavior.

The Spine to Body Infection

Spine operation gone wrong: In the summer of 2010, my back started to show its age. Instead of standing straight, I was starting to bend forward.

> While I was dancing at a casino, one of the women commented, "You look like a little old lady out there dancing." I was so embarrassed that I took action. My primary doctor referred me to the top spine surgeon at the one of the nearby hospitals. MRI's were taken, and a plan was made. "Success is the norm, but you never know," the doctors said.

I elected to have the operation and shave bone from the L-4 and L-5 vertebra and take pressure off the sciatic nerve. Dates were set for the second week in February 2011 and the initial exploratory preps were done.

> The night before the surgery, out of the blue, Jennifer came to my hospital room. She asked me to not to have the operation, at least now. She felt something was not right. Jennifer was so upset, the nurses allowed her to stay the night; if you believe in foresight or a higher power, there it was. The operation took place the next morning. The hospital provided me with two days of in-patient recovery and then I was discharged.

Within one week I developed an infection in the lower spine and was readmitted. A second operation took place immediately. Events and circumstances took place as I faded away.

The Worcester Hospital medical report read:

- Neuro-encephalopathy

- Congestive heart failure

- Cardiomyopathy

- Sepsis

- Sinus tachycardia

- Circulatory failure

- Neurologic failure

- Renal failure

- Hematologic failure

- Severe metabolic derangement

- Overwhelming infection

The procedures to address the infection and the initial botched operation included:

- three more operations

- two full-body blood transfusions

- two induced comas

- flooding the body with antibiotics

In late March, I woke and the first thing I heard was the ICU nurse announcing, "He is going to live."

When I could walk, talk, and drive again, I went back to visit the ICU nurses, twice. They called me "blue eyes." More than ever, I believe doctors do not save a patient! It is the nurses who save a patient!

Friends and family: Once I was taken off life support, my cognitive abilities slowly came back. Though I couldn't speak, I could listen and remember. Johnny had visited me once and lost it while he was at the hospital. Johnny could not accept seeing his once strong dad lying in a bed with machines allowing him to breath. Other than one visit from my brother, no family visited, and other friends were barred from the ICU.

My only other visitor was my brother, James. James was the fourth child of Anna and Jack Masters; I was the fifth. James was the brother who would sit in front of the TV with me and watch cowboy shows on Saturday morning. As we moved through life, he married Clare and they had two daughters who later would become teachers. As James rose in the executive ranks with income to match, so did I. We were close.

In April and May 2011, I was placed in two rehabilitation centers. The first was the Boltonville Rehabilitation Center. If I could move my head I was lucky. I turned it enough to see the person next to me being stripped, rolled in the bed sheet and placed on a gurney. The short guy in the Celtic shirt had died. At that time, I was paralyzed with meds being fed to me by Caribbean nurses. Existence at Boltonville was awful! My brother James, who had stood over me and watch tears flow out of my eyes, moved me to a different rehabilitation facility in Westboro, just one mile from my house. There I learned to walk, talk, and perform activities of daily life such as making it to the bathroom and cleaning up the shit I spilled on the floor. The antibiotic treatment lasted until September of 2011 and renal control was regained in October 2011.

Jennifer was often absent. She would come for a short visit or meet me for drinks. Our day trips and weekend getaways were a thing of the past. Slowly, and without my realizing it, Jennifer was gravitating towards a different crowd. It was a remake of the spring and summer of 2007--people with money getting together and having a good time. Barry, a good-looking man whom everyone liked, was a regular figure around town. Of course, I introduced Barry and Jennifer. It was Brian Masters who was now struggling. I wasn't a millionaire anymore.

My activities were limited to working on the lawn, pool, house, internet job searches, and drinking in front of the TV. Family and friends were hundreds of miles away and knew nothing of these experiences; they had their own lives.

Again, I mention the role of abstinence from sex when in recovery. The reason is very straightforward. Whether it is with a man, woman, or same sex partner, without even wanting to a sexual relationship can cause disruption of recovery and clear-headed decisions.

The Highlights of the Remaining Part of 2011

• Watching two women argue at my bedside about who had authority over my estate.

- Faking the medical staff into believing I had more of everything I needed be released.

- Being driven to an appointment to see the head of Infectious Diseases of the university hospital. "You are a miracle," he said. "Fifty percent die, forty percent are in wheel chair with catheter, five percent walk and talk functionally, and five percent are you," he said.

- Realizing that almost no one knew I was away or even cared.

- Being without visitors to make me feel normal and no one to provide the truths.

It is easy to look back and ask, "What should I have done, or could I have done?" My choice was not to look for support but to tackle the problems by myself. My choice was to look to the old habits that made me happy and feel in control. Earlier, I said that education, solid friends, and family support combined with medical assistance are needed for recovery. At your crisis point, what would you do?

The Contributors' Overall Impact

The financial impact: In 2011, there was no income coming in and all bills were being paid by money drawn from my 401s and IRAs. This lasted through 2012 and part of 2013. I sold the house that I bought back from Linda, leaving only $25,000 in my bank account. I analyzed my assets and liabilities. From what I could see, with an alimony of 20% of all gross income, I had no hope.

Earnings Record, Social Security Statement, Earnings Record, Social Security

Year	Taxed Social Security Earnings	Taxed Medicare Earnings
2008	$100,178	$100,178
2009	$106,800	$118,694

2010	$75,279	$75,279
2011	$0	$0
2012	$9,902	$9,902
2013	$3,826	$3,826
2014	$5,853	$5,853
2015	$1,927	$1,927

Liabilities

Creditor	Nature of Debt	Year Incurred	Amount Due
IRS	2012 Capital Gain	2012	$17,650
RI Tax	2010 taxes	2010	$1,823
MA State	2012 taxes	2012	$1,290
Bank of America	Credit Card	2013	$19,490
Shrewsbury Cable	Electric/Cable	2013	$643
Capital One	Credit Card	2013	3,546
First Financial	Credit Card	2013	$1,763
Midland Fund	Credit Card	2014	$3,813
Town Moving	Westborough Storage	2014	$0*
Wells Fargo	Car Loan	2015	$3,813
Total			$53,425

*Westborough Storage settled and forgave my $10,000 debt

The emotional impact: I was totally alone to make choices. To me, I was normal, and I could continue to function as I had in the past. As the money dissipated Jennifer chose to be "friends with benefits." The other women moved in and out of my life only to address their loneliness, not mine.

I was not normal on the job search front either. The medical community failed to tell me that it would take at least a year or two for the tremors to go away and a full recovery. In early 2012, I was shaking uncontrollably, so I would self-medicate. But, if you try to act normal and think you are normal, disappointment is inevitable. It became a vicious cycle leading to depression, loneliness, and anxiety. I was fooling myself every day.

> In early August 2012, Peter Smith and his wife came from LA to Boston to move his son into his apartment on Boylston Street. I was to meet the family at the Copley Plaza for dinner. Peter Smith had been my friend since we were five years old. We went to Syracuse University and Peter was in my wedding. I attempted to reduce my fear and anxiety by having drinks at the bar prior to meeting them. The bottom line is that my conversation was that of another person. I embarrassed myself and the family. My relationship with the Smiths was never the same.

This was me, not you. But everything is relative. The problems or events that come at us seem insurmountable. In your mind, yours could be just as bad as mine. We need to understand that our future outcomes of addiction, because it is addiction, may be the same. You'll see that when we reach the portion of this book where I tell you about institutionalization. Everyone is the same.

Masking Contributors - The Short Hard Fall

The Pattern of Addictive Behaviors Exposed

Trying again without professional help: In early 2013, I started to act:

- Set firm times to attend AA meetings

- Started dating a woman who had no drama--again

- Went to regular medical appointments and checkups

- Returned to Martial Arts as an instructor and student

- Taught myself how to play tennis and bowl again

- Did not drink near the time of a job interview

- Still met people for drinks and dinner

Now, I analyzed what was done and what was not done correctly. It may be hindsight, but seeking addiction education and learning from someone else's experiences is what "prevention recovery" is about. I did none of the self-help activities and continued my old behaviors. What I allowed to happen to me is not at all pretty

As I look back on those times, AA meetings were great. The people were not afraid to put their hearts on the table, and they were willing to help. The important start to AA is to really listen to others; to learn from them. I befriended Tom Lacey, a selectman from my town. Tom became my sponsor and over time told me good words of wisdom. "If the bad experiences have not happened yet, such as no money and credit, they will. You need to realize you hit bottom. It is important to pair up with a sponsor, so you can stay away from substance abuse and get another's perspective. It is important to understand that attending meetings is not a passing grade; it is not a requirement to graduate."

As I started to investigate solutions to masking problems with a substance, I was only exposed to one piece of the puzzle in recovery. The future would educate me about the need for multiple assistance. Unfortunately, I had lacked that education. At the same time, I was dealing with the most common internal belief, "this could not happen to me."

> But looking for the opposite sex or partner with no drama does not stop the past from catching up. Lori Schwartz, who had no drama, begged me to stay in Massachusetts, so, I renewed the lease for my apartment and continued supporting her needs. Eight am and eight pm phone calls were a must for Lori if she were to have a stable day. It was also amazing that Jennifer and Sherry found out where I lived and made a point of showing up unannounced with the offer of meals, drinking, or sex. It got scary when they would ring the neighbors' bell to gain access to the building or call me from outside, too drunk to drive. I started to resume my old patterns of cohabitating when needed.

Interviewing for jobs: Just being sober when preparing and attending interviews does not mean something else is not going to get in the way of a positive outcome. I had excellent meetings at two major software companies. The analytics I would have to sell were compelling, and I knew exactly how to talk to the C level executives to make the sale. My brain said, "See, I can do it again." Then the talent manager would bring the bad news; the real news is that you are too old. Substance use would come right back to calm my depression and induce feelings of the good old times. A Catch-22.

Within a relative short period of time my irrational actions sealed my future.

> During the first week of February 2013, I arranged a phone interview with a Vice President of Sales. My voice sounded drunk and I lost a potential $90,000 a year, plus commission job. This was a sales position that at any other time in my life would have taken me to the top.

Irrational behavior and self-pity led me to disrupt my activities such as karate. There were no repercussions. Money became tighter which meant the much needed ninety days stay in a hospital or therapy center never happened. When everything began to collapse, Lori Schwartz was no help. Her attitude was, you are on your own. Yet, she still wanted me to call her twice a day to talk. Because of my relationship with Lori, I lost four months of time and money.

Liquidation and storage: I hired a moving and storage company to take my furniture and belongings to their secured bins. Then I called my niece Jane and her husband Greg for help. Jane is a diehard Masters who watches over two centuries of history of the Masters' family. I called them, explained the situation, and they were on their way. By the time Jane and Greg were in Massachusetts, my shakes and the slurring of my words were apparent.

On a Saturday afternoon, Jane and Greg packed all the remaining oriental rugs, mahogany tables, wide screen TVs, suits and shirts, pictures, trophies, and my sailing ships that I made by hand. Everything would be taken to their home in Skaneateles, New York and would be returned to me when I could get back on my feet.

Scream for financial help: One of my last actions at that time was to email selected friends and family asking for financial help. It was obvious that I needed food, shelter, and gas; gas was closing in on

$4.40 per gallon. The email was specific that anything given to me at any time was a loan; the loan would be paid back once I landed a position. Since my reputation was still intact, I felt that most people would understand my circumstances. To ask for financial help in such a way was the most heart-wrenching thing I ever had to do. But pride was not an option. Attempting suicide was not an option.

For me, the ability to store what I had left and make that scream for financial assistance was the only chance I had. For you or others, there may be no such option. This could mean that your time line towards substance use rock bottom could be faster.

My Downward Spiral of Addictive Behaviors

This New World with No True Home Begins

Within ten months, I lost control of the lifestyle I had been used to, I had to use the money and assets I had to provide shelter. I tried to reach out to those "bar room friends" to help me and as a result heard my first "no" from them but I really didn't care. The result was that I had to look to the state for transitional assistance including money, food stamps, shelter options, and transportation. Was this the rock bottom that people talk about?

At the end of July 2013, my Toyota was packed to the hilt. The passenger seat was left open for a rider, food, my brief case, note pads, a file, and cell phone. The back seats and hatch back carried my laptop, printer, files, summer clothes, jackets, two suitcases, and a suit bag filled with everything for a professional job interview. The car was alcohol free since, at this point, I was very sensitive about drinking and driving.

The first day of homelessness: The actual feeling in your mind and body, that you are truly without a roof over your head, is impossible to describe. Each moment becomes surreal and you are 100 percent alone. The brain is moving 100 miles an hour for a direction, but there is none. Everything or anything depends on the charity of others.

Reaching out to friends I helped in the past: The library was my choice as a place to go and think things out. I thought about the people I had helped in years past. What about the young adults I had taken out of cocaine houses? My thoughts went to the Easter Sunday after I had come back to my house from the hospital. I met many people leaving church. There was the family who spent time at my lake house and whose daughter I physically removed from a known cocaine house in Worcester. They were as cold as ice. Then, Barry came over to say hello and said, "How glad I am that you lived." No, not Barry! I realized that he knew my confidential information from only one person--Jennifer! What an Easter Sunday.

What about the women who were always at my door? What about Jennifer, who had been my partner? Jennifer's divorce was finished, and she got the house in Vermont, the house in Southborough, the four time-shares, jewelry, two cars, furniture, and alimony. When I called for help, her answer was, "No, I am seeing my friend." Now, what about Sherry? I had been there for her after breast cancer. Sherry fought Jennifer for control of my estate, and her son liked me a lot. I called Sherry from the steps of the library and asked if I could stay at her apartment. Her words were, "You have to be kidding. My family would not like it at all; even one night could be a problem!" I felt weak at the knees and as if I had been kicked in the gut. I was alone.

During this time, I called every friend I had who might have room and provide a temporary roof over my head. I thought of Bob Fitter, whom I knew was an alcoholic; he had old New England money, which kept him from going under financially. Bob had been a so-called friend for two decades, but, at the beginning of my divorce I saw messages on my wife's answering machine with his name. I bit the bullet and called him anyway. I received no answer. I called Jeff Lent, who gave me his house when he went to France. He had an open house due to his divorce. No answer. I called Dick Able. Dick and his family benefited from the Network Group I created to help get him a job and save his wife who had multiple sclerosis; he said he had no room because his son was moving in. I called Terri Halford, whose son I took in for free for four months in 2010 because Terri's boyfriend lived in a town with a bad school system. No answer.

Stigma: Then it hit me like a brick. This was my first taste of "stigma." No matter who you were or what you had accomplished, current events worked against you. "Brian is broke and is a drunk." Some people were happy to see me this way; it is human nature. And then there are those whom you never expected would give you that type of treatment. Crying does not fix anything, but I cried anyway.

First taste of social services dependency: Finally, two of my closest friends stepped up to help. Mike and Liz Garrison allowed me to live at their house for two months. They provided positive support I spoke about. Mike, Liz, and I knew that a December hire would be unrealistic, so Mike and I concentrated on getting me unemployment, food stamps, and a health plan. Mike pushed me to get done what needed to be done--a total reliance on the transitional systems from the state.

I remembered the middle- and upper-income people I had met over the decades. Many of them would make comments about cutting the programs for the homeless. They would say, "Why pay for these losers?" I guess, now I was one of them--a loser!

Depression was a constant companion, and I was losing the ability to stay sober. By the end of December, I needed a new base of operations to stay alive; the Garrisons had done enough. I made phone calls asking for financial help and my immediate family came to my aid once they confirmed my attempted sobriety at the Garrisons'. Now I moved to a New England bed and breakfast Inn within a different town. I had arranged a rent of $600 per month, which was paid by my brothers. My first night there, I raised my voice to a man at the bar and was shut off for the rest of my stay. I had not appreciated what I had.

The Inn: The place I was staying is a quaint New England rent-a-room by the night, week, or month style of business. The rooms were clean and spacious; every inch felt like the 1800s except for the bathroom, elevator, and restaurant. Even the floorboards under the carpets would squeak as you walked down the hall. The inn was owned and run by Tom and Lori Black. These two people were the nicest man and woman known across two towns. Tom and Lori both had blue eyes, blond hair, fair skin, and were good looking. To top it off, they were high school sweethearts. The restaurant business was their dream and a successful one. They were great to me.

Remember when Randy Landers attacked me the day before Thanksgiving and ran out the VFW door? After it was all over and in the past, the cleaning lady told me that it was one of the Black's restaurant rooms that Randy hid out in to avoid the police. Here was the drama I so much wanted to avoid. I was circling back to the people and places that helped me drink the pain away. And I did. With the comfort of a place to stay, I lapsed into complacency! Without help from multiple sources, any alcoholic and drug user will relapse because of complacency.

But I did not seek out medical help. I didn't make any attempt to stop the pain in my brain.

Life on the road: I decided it was time to step back from my false hopes and stand strong. I left the inn and relieved my friends and family from paying rent. My car became my home and I learned the art of dodging the police and the repo man sent by Wells Fargo.

While staying at the inn, I had learned to frequent food pantries for needed supplies. Now I had to occupy my days by going to libraries and hanging out in large apartment complex parking lots. Gas and needed supplies came from weekly paychecks from two jobs that I held. I had a job as a limo driver and as a driver at one of New England's largest auction houses. Baths consisted of getting into a McDonalds or Burger King before the truckers did. I would carry a change of clothes in a bag, cover my face with my hat and get to the bathroom before the staff spotted me. If I was fortunate to be alone, I would hang the clothes, wash my hair and private parts, change my clothes, and head for the car. As time went on, I became an expert.

It kind of ruins your thought of a clean restroom, doesn't it?

The first quarter of 2014 was gone, and I had not made any significant strides to improve my physical, economic, and mental condition. My days seemed to repeat each other, which allowed depression to work on me daily. It became a game to see how I could break the boredom with free handouts -- in other words, begging. Occasionally, the local movie theater had slow evenings, and I needed shelter from the cold. That meant the ticket associates couldn't care less if a man, dressed conservatively, and commenting that he had no money, was allowed in to see a free movie. When the movie ended, I moved to the movie next door. So, I had two movies for the price of "0;" more important, I was occupied and warm. The ticket takers would allow me this luxury once or twice a month. The grocery stores and restaurants I used to visit became places to pick up free meals and a drink. Gas was $4.50 a gallon, so driving two towns over was not affordable. It is amazing how your mind starts to look at things. Every quarter added up to a dollar. Every dollar meant almost a quarter gallon of gas. So, anytime I thought of spending money, I thought about what that money meant in gas. Food intake was at a minimum and I quickly moved from wine to cheap vodka, consumed at my present home, my parked car.

The body begins to fail: Then came the physical realization that my time had ended. One of my two jobs were at a car auction house in Framingham. One day, while lining up cars for the general inspection and photo shoots, something in me failed. I took the car out of park and put my foot on the gas pedal, slowly moving the car forward. When I went for the brake pedal, the car kept moving. Though I kept pushing the brake, the car never stopped, barely missing my friend who was taking pictures at the time.

After failing to stop the car, I would check the foot daily for sensitivity of the toes, foot and calf. Then it happened, the tingling in my right foot became numbness. I was experiencing neuropathy because of the botched surgery. I didn't experience any problems when I was driving my car every day, but what about the auction house cars and more important, the limo vans I drove at my primary job. I didn't want to lose that job--it brought in the most money and steady hours. I could not allow myself to ignore an issue that could harm others while I oversaw their safety. My decision was a no brainer. I left both jobs and wiped out the only income for which I did not have to beg.

My time in New England had run out. In 1982, I had come to Massachusetts to make a name and become wealthy. I had accomplished my goals and then some. Now, thirty-two years later, changes had to be made along with a new course of action. I decided California was the place I ought to be.

I picked California because after my son graduated from the university he moved to Los Angeles. The picture I had in my mind for years was visiting him by plane. But circumstances dictated that I was to drive 3000 miles by car: I was unsure of its ability make it from Boston to New York, let alone to Los Angeles. Most of all, the last thing I wanted was for Johnny to see me broke and suffering from depression and alcoholism. But the brain does not see the consequences of its actions if the irrational parts of the brain are still in control.

Changing the Environment by Running Away

My trip to New York: In late April 2014, I repacked the car and gathered enough money to get to central New York State. I did not realize my pills for cholesterol, depression, blood pressure, and anxiety where part of the equation. I packed whatever I had at the time. Hell, every state in the union has a CVS, right?

The first stop was the home of my friends Hank and Lisa Fox. This couple has been friends of mine since 1978. Both went to the same New York State university, along with Mike Garrison. Lisa and Hank fell in love, married, raised three young adults, and established an excellent reputation in their town. There was no judging or drama in the Fox household. For two days, I could laugh, go to church, bars, and be with down-to-earth people.

My second stop was at Jim and May Goodman's house not too far from where the Lisa and Hank lived. Jim has been a friend since high school. He owned a farm as well as a meat scale business. His wife, May, owned a Chinese restaurant. Together, they built a cash business and an estate worth seven figures. I was extremely happy for Jim. Being a former car mechanic, Jim was able to ready my car for the ride west. There was no cost to me, just an understanding that I would try to get better.

My last stop was Skaneateles, a quaint little town on a beautiful lake in the Finger Lakes Region of New York. My brother Jack lived in the village with his wife Beth and adult children. Jane, their daughter had married Greg, a Navy officer. Greg, I was to realize later, is a standup guy. He did not have to be a Brian Masters fan, but he stood with Jane and welcomed me back. As a family, we planned my trip across the country via Route 70. Going west was not a new experience for me. In 1978, after I graduated from Syracuse University I hitchhiked out west before taking a computer sales job. I loved the people, the places, and the experiences; that excited me for the trip.

Since my plans were to start again in California, I reclaimed two oriental rugs from the property Jane and Greg had been storing for me. One rug for Johnny, and one rug for me. People gave me cash and food cards to make the trip.

This is another juncture when I could have had a great chance to address my addiction. My friend Jim Goodman had told me about a facility in central New York. It was a brand new and state of the art treatment center for PTSD, depression, and substance use. This would have been a good place for me. Later on in time, when I read my medical records from my Primary Care doctor, Dr. Ford, I found I was diagnosed with, "Situational Anxiety," just short of a true PSTD diagnosis. In time, I would realize Dr. Ford had done me a favor due the stigma of PSTD. I could not fight anxiety and fear, so I drank alcohol every day. Unfortunately, the stigma of PTSD was strong in the United States in 2014. Victims would avoid admitting they had the disease caused by trauma due to its stigma. People fear what they do not understand.

Road trip: The Toyota and I shuffled towards Buffalo at 7 am. I took the truck route west and it became apparent that sleeping at rest stops was acceptable. In other words, it was less likely that the police would bother you. When I reached Kansas, I met truckers who were slightly younger than myself. We had some drinks at a stop, then went our own way. Except I decided to buy some "roadies" for the drive, just like the other men. Hell, I had been in control for weeks.

You can change the environment, but it will not change the problem. I was bringing all my emotional baggage with me. Dysfunction increases ten times when you cut off old medication; unknown to me you can physically kill yourself. Liz Garrison had once told me, "Never take yourself off depression pills in one day. The consequences are very bad." Liz never explained how bad it was, and I did not care to ask at that point.

I decided to stop all medication other than the blood pressure and cholesterol pills. By, Denver, my mood became euphoric, and I was enhancing the feeling with wine in a cup.

> As I was driving, my mind wandered back to July 1978, when I was a 22-year-old, hitchhiking the highway outside of Albuquerque, New Mexico. I was picked up by a gentleman in a brand-new Cadillac. He asked me to drive so he could get some sleep. After the gentleman woke up from his "black out," he asked me to take the exit for gas and beer. It was then I realized the beer was a twelve pack of Budweiser and a bottle of scotch from the trunk. When we hit the Flagstaff, Arizona rest stop, the man got out of the car and started urinating on the side of a building. How utterly clueless I was about alcohol or the disease. I ordered him food, took his credit card, got him a room, and put him to bed at the hotel. All my life, when I thought back to the man in the brand-new car, I said, "I would never be that man."

The Brian Masters of 2014 could never even remotely resemble that man! But after the Rockies and a clear shot to LA, the wine became more frequent and the medication less and less. Johnny met me at a gas station. There was a cup full of wine in the holder and a half a box of wine behind the passenger seat.

I had reached that point where an addict will perform acts without any regard for the feelings of others. If a family member or friend hits that point, medical attention is needed.

A stab at making it work: I can never, really, recover from the shame of what happened when I got to LA. But again, I put a plan into action:

•	I set up a schedule at AA in Hollywood and immediately got a sponsor

•	I set up the computer with all the job sites to feed me opportunities

•	I accessed the local food pantry on a limited basis

•	Johnny looked at apartments for us

Johnny found a job for me at Google Shopping Express (GSE), which was beta testing home delivery with Los Angeles as the first city. The objective was to compete against Amazon's home delivery. I loved the $10 per hour job. My Latino co-workers treated me fine and an LA blond with looks to kill joined the group. I was sober, and they were stoned.

Stigma can come in smells: When you are homeless, eating and hygiene become art forms. A fast food restaurant restroom is a combined changing room, shower, and bathroom. Sanitizer is your deodorant for parts of your body and face. During my evaluation period at GSE, all my test deliveries with management went extremely well. Except the final test day; the mood felt different. The next morning, when I called my manager for new orders, I was told that they smelled alcohol on me during my last trial day. At the same time, management realized that my Toyota was only a two-door and had a gouge on the side. They wanted four-door vehicles without dents. Therefore, I was not Google material. Having been a successful executive with a six-figure income, being let go from a $10 an hour job was no less than total humiliation.

Stopping prescribed medication? It can kill you: My thoughts were running wild. Depression and anxiety were coming at me relentlessly, so I went to the store for vodka because it masked the mental pain and calmed my shaking. I failed again to realize that I had not taken any of the medication I was prescribed eight years ago and had taken every day since. I began hallucinating that my leg was turning blue, so I called 911. One day later, Johnny issued "tough love" by asking me to leave. Hollywood is a small town and the last thing he needed was a dad who could ruin his career. Peter Smith, my best friend for life, who lived in LA, handed me money for the ride home. Peter and his family had been in Boston at the Copley Plaza when I embarrassed myself years earlier. I gave my son the oriental rug, my family ring, and I hit the road. I wanted to die.

An interesting fact that I have learned from the scholars I have met, and my own research is that programs such as DARE, Scared Straight, JUST SAY NO, and Tough Love were all failures. They had the opposite effect or shorten a person's life.

For the benefit of the doubt! Was it me who, in the back of my mind, could not face being the strong father helping his son? I was the one who had to relocate and start from scratch, like a boy in his 20's but really in his late 50's. It was my son saying, "I will get you a place and a job." Maybe I just threw up my hands at the first gate and committed mental suicide.

The Street

A quiet ride with nowhere to go: The sun was rising, revealing the smog in the morning light. It was my good luck that I took the southern exit east instead of the middle route east. If I were to give anyone advice about the most beautiful views from an interstate highway, it would be Route 40. From the mountains of east California through Nevada, the colors and rock formations are spectacular. The blues and reds dazzle your eyes. Your depth perception is useless; what you think is one mile might be ten miles, and the only way to know is to get out of the car and walk. I once stopped to take in the view of a valley colored red and where Route

40 has no guard rails and a 600-foot drop. Purposely, I stuck my thoughts into a void, got back in the car, and just drove.

With the money that Peter had given me, funds transferred to me a month earlier by Martin Phillips and my job money, I could make it back to central New York. It was amazing that I still had Subway cards from Jane and Greg, so I could eat. The truck stops were the same and the music was dull. My desire to drink alcohol was at a minimum, so my habit became Red Bull to stay awake. I decided to cut north to position myself to hit the New York State Thruway and the Finger Lakes Region. Jane and Greg made my day by prepaying a hotel room in South Bend, Indiana, one block from Notre Dame university, home of Notre Dame football, and the spirit of Rudy who also graduated in 1978. It gave me the positive boost I needed not to simply stop and get lost some place.

The last straw: It was the second week of June 2014 when I drove into Skaneateles. I knew in my heart that my brother James had learned of my behavior in Hollywood from Johnny, and James would have passed the information on to Jack and family. I was not sure what to expect from my family in New York. My brother Jack is the oldest of the family and has always been verbally direct. He was also a police officer, so if there was any chance that I had PTSD, it was a risk for me to stay at Jack's house due to the N.Y. Police Association's belief, "PSTD, no firearms." Who knew what Jane and Greg might say?

My memories of New York State, friends and family, were everything to me. It was my foundation. New York's places and affiliations were part of my being. It did not take much time to realize that my character was close to being destroyed and support would be gone. Within an hour of turning the engine off, I was told that my membership at the country club my father had help found was gone, along with any sympathy for me as an alcoholic. It was a whirlwind of conversations and innuendos that my tired ass could not comprehend. At that point, I broke down and left.

It is apparent that Step One of AA had been accomplished. Other than the car and the possessions in it, I had nothing left but myself. Though that might not be the truth, it is the way I saw it. There is one reality in AA methodology you can bet on: "When you are powerless over alcohol-and your lives are unmanageable," it is time to step up. It just depends how you want to do it.

Now I was back on the New York Thruway looking for a place to rest my head and see things more clearly. Hank and Lisa put me up for a few days. Staying with them gave me the time to research Massachusetts housing for the homeless. A sad joke was that I had told my brother Jack in November 2013 that *I would be dead before going into a shelter*. Six months later, I was focused on a shelter outside of Boston hoping they would have a bed. The car was gassed and ready to go. While on the road, I decided not to make any more stops and head directly to the shelter. What could possibly happen now?

I was headed to Framingham, just three towns over from Westborough, where I had raised my son. Once off the Massachusetts Turnpike, I traveled Route 9 and through my old town to get to my destination. All the memories of playing with Johnny in the pool came rushing back. Johnny's graduation from high school and him being named Prom King. Golfing at the country club. Being presented with my Black Belt and feeling no fear. Once I wiped the tears from my eyes, I refocused on the road. Then, out of nowhere came the beautiful blue and red lights of a Southborough, police car.

"Mr. Masters, your registration has expired as of two days ago. Were you aware of that?" The tow truck was called, and the police officer told me I could take what I could carry! "Do you have a friend to call?" I watched the last of everything I owned being hooked to the truck. The driver was nice enough to take me within a half-mile of the hotel. I was lucky enough that my credit card still had money for a one-night stay. I was fortunate enough that the hotel was the spot for hookers and traveling men. The hookers drove me to the liquor store I had frequented, as another person, a hundred times. Before I passed out watching the TV, I called good old Mike Garrison.

Well, there it is. June 26th. I watched the last of my possessions being towed away and I had no money to retrieve them. I had one suitcase, one brief case, and the clothes on my back.

The next morning, I got sick to my stomach and had a head that wanted me to die. My body was shaking, my face was white, my eyes were red, and I needed water badly. My mind could not take depression, fear, and total loss any more. When Mike got to the door, I held myself up against the bathroom wall and said, "I have to know why? I must know why I drink and why I am depressed. I want to commit myself." Mike's response was, "It is about time."

Transition I

This is the crossover. I committed myself to a substance abuse hospital to attack depression and the addiction to alcohol head on. I wanted to win against this invisible monster. At this point, I had to admit that my head could not grasp it all. I had used cocaine, alcohol, and sometimes pot over the decades. The drugs never came close to impeding my rational thinking. Even as money came in the door, cocaine, the social drug of the time, and the sexual euphoria it created did not take control. But between 2011 and 2014, I had hit a wall.

The first part of this book is meant to help you to understand the environment, the people I had known, and my spiral downward. I have shared with you my most personal experiences, which molded my behavior. Once you are in this world, you are on a level playing field with everyone. It is up to each person to decide his or her next steps. I had my ups and downs; some were my fault, and some were pushed upon me. Each person has his ups and downs, and they can be just as important to that individual as mine were to me. Now, I will open other memories and other people's memories to get you close to street reality. Going forward you will meet various men and women, the institutions, the housing, the streets, and the people's hatred and self-hatred of this environment. You will also encounter the hope that keeps people alive.

My intent is to get you close to a reality you may not have known before. I know that I had no clue about it nor do most of the people I know. But it is important for you to see the reality, because you may have the opportunity to change your own or someone else's collision course, once this world is exposed.

Remember what I said, "everyone's experiences are unique". I used only alcohol as my substance. Alcohol, meth, opiates, and other drugs are now included when I refer to substance use as it pertains to the subculture. Multiple "contributors" came into my life; maybe

42

only one will touch you. Either way there could be an effect that leads to negative outcome. As you read, I hope you will walk in my shoes and identify with me. The severity of it all is life ending. It will take different and multiple techniques to stabilize, control, and overcome this disease. Then you and anyone else can move on.

I said earlier, "Someone needs to let people know what is going on out here before it happens to them." Well, this is the start of what you need to know.

Interlude

In the first part of the book, I described actual events including the friends, family, and others who touched my life. Much of that content will be carried into the next two sections of this book. I'll also discuss the more scientific and research-based aspects of addiction, trauma, and recovery as well as describe my experiences on the street and in shelters. Here's a list of aspects of substance use you should keep in mind as we move on. A full description of each is in the appendix.

- Parts of the Brain and Their Roles in Addiction

- Housing and Shelters Defined

- A Technique for Combating Triggers

Phase 2--
The Institutions-The Housing-The Shelters-The Streets

Excruciation-Entered with Eyes Wide Open

Preparation - The Garrisons' knowledge transfer: I was sitting on the curb outside the motel room and I heard Mike on his cell phone talking with Liz.

"He has decided to commit himself. Yes. Yes. He is going to need a day or so to get to the hospital. Okay!"

All was good with Liz, who was understanding but was not open to my staying with them for a long time. Thank God, she said, "Yes."

My mind was focused on "commitment." It was as if I entered the neutral zone. I was not in command, nor did I want to be. All forward thinking and memories of past events were halted. As far as I was concerned, Mike was in charge, so I did not want to interfere, especially since I did not know what to do or where to go.

Mike knew the Massachusetts health system process after throwing himself into the system nine years earlier. A mutual friend of ours, Alex Crown, had a teenage son who stepped into the heroin subculture. Mike took it upon himself to work with Alex to save his son's life. It took years of trial and error attempts at either intervention or institutionalization. Mike's intervention involved street level episodes, which increased his knowledge of the environment. After, literally, years of blood, sweat, and tears, everyone was successful. The experience put Mike in a position to know where I should start.

The difference in the process, next steps, and mindset is age and experience. I was involved with alcohol, not heroin, and my life experience was mature. It is at this point the health system process became my lifeline. I warn you, the give and take between all parties created the hell I hope you will learn from.

We drove to Mike's home, so he could get back to his job. I could clean up and eat, but the wine abuse from the night before was ripping my mind apart. Tylenol was not enough to bring the body back to a somewhat stable condition, so I would occasionally drink a mixed vodka and orange juice. This allowed me to work with Mike on retrieving the car and its contents.

When we pulled up to the house, the sun was shining, the temperature was eighty degrees, and the Garrison dogs were barking. It was like a scene from the Donna Reed show of the 60's. "Well, which hospital do you want to go to?" Mike asked. I picked one that had a very good reputation in Massachusetts and was right in the middle of one of the richest towns within the Route 128 belt. I felt that if I were to commit myself, at least I would have a chance at an upscale next step. Plus, Mike was familiar with it.

On the way to the hospital, Mike told me what to expect when we arrived. At the registration desk, I would tell them that I have a drug problem, depression, and I could potentially *hurt myself*. But there was no way I would admit that I had any intention of suicide! Even though I had thought of it, that was then, and this was now. But in the health system, suicide risk is the most common way to move into an institution for help. While sitting at the intake meeting, I told the nurse my issues; it was Mike who commented about the thoughts of hurting myself. It was if there was a silent understanding; everyone agreed, and a blue band was put around my wrist.

Now that the formalities were done, Mike asked if I could be sent to a good facility. The nurse looked at my collared shirt, khaki shorts, short socks, and Docksiders shoes; she said, "Pembrook would be the best for Brian." Mike and I said thank you and walked into the waiting room. Mike went to the car and made business calls while I watched TV. I did not have *any idea* that I would not be allowed such a simple thing as TV viewing once I was institutionalized. Mike grabbed my carry bag from the car and came back to the waiting room.

The bag contained the following:

- Two changes of clothes

- Bathroom toiletries for my teeth and hair

- No sharp objects of any kind

- No shoes with laces

- No belts

- Only one or two days of prescribed drugs

- My cell phone and charger

"Everything else will be provided for you at the hospital", Mike said.

The ambulance pulled up at the door and my name was called. My wristband was checked by the nurse and then by the driver. I was told to lie on the gurney for the trip and I quickly moved into the ambulance with my carry-on bag.

Mike stood at the end of the ambulance, told me he and Liz would come and visit, and waved goodbye.

Institutionalization

Admittance to Pembrook

The ride: The gurney was angled, so I could view our trip toward Cape Cod. The 128 traffic was thinning down because it was 9:30 in the morning. Still, some cars were zooming by at 80 or 90 miles an hour. I loved watching it. I read the names of the businesses that lined the highway and those brought back memories of past computer sales. I thought of Haemonetics, whose sign could be seen from the road, and the Sheraton where I had closed slightly over one million dollars in sales over the last decade.

As we turned right at the Route 3 sign, the businesses and cars went away. Most cars had been heading to Boston, while I was headed south toward the Cape. The trees got smaller as we approached the Cape and I could smell the ocean blowing inland. We took the Plymouth exit, then turned on the ambulance lights. In no time, we pulled into the emergency entrance and parked. We had arrived.

Physical items: When I entered the in-patient facility, my control and choices were limited. Being in a Rehab facility is short of being in jail. First, I attended an intake meeting with a nurse and aide. The nurse reviewed with me what the hospital had documented, and *I authorized* admittance. At that point, the vocal tone of the staff changed into one of being *"matter of fact."* As Mike had warned me, my personal bag was laid out on a table and each article was searched one by one. The bathroom kit had a small pouch that I had for years and never traveled without. Since the pouch contain a small scissor for nose hair, the kit was confiscated, along with my cell phone, charger, and all my medications prescribed by my primary physician. I was given a hospital bathroom packet, hospital pants, and a pullover. Then I signed for all the items given and taken.

Self-diagnosis: My second meeting was with the nurse and a resident doctor. It was my chance to explain to the medical staff what I felt the problems were. I stated,

- Alcohol abuse to mask depression and pain

- Depression

- Acute loneliness

I provided a history that included the contributors, the shunning by my sister, her family, Mike's brother, and potentially my son.

I made it very clear that I had entered their program voluntarily. My immediate and long-term needs, in my opinion, were a clear understanding of the causes of depression and professional help to eliminate the need for alcohol.

The most amazing feeling came over me while at the intake meeting; I felt relief. Instead of talking to friends and family like Mike, Hank, and James, I was discussing what I thought was important with outsiders. I knew that I was isolated from the outside, and I felt protected.

The nurse and doctor wrote their notes and explained to me that I would have meetings with their resident psychiatrist and internal medicine doctor. I was told that my other medications were to be given to me *in the ward.*

Ward? That was a term that I only heard on TV.

Ward?

Merriam Webster defines a ward as a person or thing under guard, protection, or surveillance, as a: a minor subject to wardship, b: a person who because of incapacity (as minority or mental illness) is under the protection of a court either directly or through a guardian appointed by the court —called also **ward** of court.

The Cambridge Advanced Learner's Dictionary defines a ward as one of the parts or large rooms into which a hospital is divided, usually with beds.

I was both! I may have been slightly hung over, depressed, and tired but my common sense and intelligence were intact. At no time had anyone described the type of hospital I was being admitted to. How were the floors divided? What were the expectations of my behavior? Who were the people I would be with? What was the role of the nursing staff? What other staff were on duty at any particular time? Again, I had no clue and I failed to ask these questions of Mike or the admitting staff. Maybe Mike did not want me to know or maybe he did not know.

The ward: I would reside on the first floor. I followed the nurse to a gray metal door, which stood out from the white walls and the tan wooden doors I saw earlier. The nurse entered the code on a pad on the wall and we could hear the sound of a bolt. She pushed the door and we walked through to what looked like a college dorm. On the left were offices and bathrooms. On the right were bedrooms with brown doors and medium-size windows above the door handle. Just before the bedrooms was a small conference room. As I walked down the hallway past the rooms and offices, I came upon a patient day room on the right and a staff medication dispensary on the left. The day room had one TV, books, chairs back against the walls, and tables in the middle; there were no windows.

Once past the patient day room was a staff room on the right connected to a small kitchen. Next was a conference room with a TV, games, and chairs. Roughly six yards beyond the conference room door was the gray door to the outside and a keypad on the wall.

The bedrooms: I was led to room 3A and B. My bed was B. I put my bag and bathroom kit on the table and sat on bed B with my hands folded. This was my home for the next two weeks unless I was deemed unfit to stay or became ill and sent to the main hospital.

The rooms had two beds, two dressers, two built in shelves, sheets, a pillow, and one blanket. Each room was spotless, and it was expected that you would keep it that way. The drawers in the dresser were private to the patient, unless it was suspected you were hoarding or had contraband brought in. I learned that staff would normally look the other way when cigarettes were hidden.

I feel it is important to mention that the Massachusetts health system may be alike or different from other health systems around the country. As we encounter the way the system approaches the needs of the patients, specifically substance use, we must keep in mind who is paying and what level of insurance an individual has. If Mike and I had not worked on applying to the Massachusetts Health System and hadn't been approved for MassHealth, the state funded insurance, none of this would be real; at least for me.

The First Days at Pembrook

This account of my first days at Pembrook are taken directly from my journal for 6-30-2014 to 7-2-2014. The notes are short and to the point. There is no privacy in a place like this. You are watched by the staff and watched by the patients. By writing, you stir the interest of all parties who will either sit next to you or stand over you. I should say, rereading my personal notes struck me hard because they were a prelude to the future.

Notes from the journal:

6-30-2014: Scared but I know I had to go to evaluation and rehabilitation.

- First Day: 9 people in the ward. 80% good people.

- 1 – 6'6' talks to himself and argues – Steve

- Linda – trying to get out here for a 7-year-old son – left today.

- Tom who tried to jump off a bridge in Attleboro. He is happy he did not and was brought here.

- They argue all the time

- Talking over the TV

- Clothes are the topic or Christian services vs. watching movie, the Passion of Christ. Violence

- No privacy

- I had to change rooms since the 6'6" black patient threatened me. He had the same issues with a woman patient.

- Big boy went nuts-banging walls. Staff calmed him down-great talent.

- Now have a new person who had been a Cape Cod lawyer, reading his summonses and verbally responding. "Over the Cuckoo Nest."

- Most are getting closer and helping those who hurt. Even 6'6" Steve

Staff is very good at defusing those yelling and screaming swear words.

What is happening to me?

- People need heavy meds and they have them. I have only LX med to help me sleep. I cannot think of the past or money.

First doctor's meetings:

Doctor: Reviewed history and feelings of why I should be here.

He had read my history and agreed: my need was detox-house to address alcohol and depression.

Social Services:

- Objective is to get me through this step and get options for next stay. A house, therapy for depression-stay away from alcohol.

- She came up with five options and we picked three.

- Therapy with outside access

- Car

- Job

Insurance must be checked for each option.

Day 3: 7-2-14:

Sleeping med is slowly wearing off. Johnny called last night. He is moving forward with a new project. He seems happy. He laughed when he heard my roommate talking to himself and my description of the Cape Cod lawyer gone nuts: broken down and talking to the walls.

Mike Garrison is coming with clothes and goodies that I can share. I am very upset that no business calls are on my cell VM.

Afternoon: I just met with the Social Worker. Good news. Could get a place in Jamaica Plain; free movement; car etc. Consulting from 1 to 5. My feeling is a job from 6 to 12 while I look for a full-time job.

6:30 pm: Tomorrow goals:

- Find out how much I owe at the bank, cell phone carrier, and insurance

- Calendar for time line

- Email on JP place

- Jane Sellers update:

- Sell my dad's shot gun-internet purchase

I had entered a system that had no differentiation of illnesses. This was a general holding facility and psychiatric hospital. I knew instinctively I was in the wrong place. The best way for me to have you start walking in my shoes is to outline a common breakdown of people, places and episodes. The people you are introduced to here will come back; they seem to circle back within the system.

The people:

Lenord: On the fourth day Lenord, a twenty-something 6'4" man, arrived. Lenord is a man that you do not want to make mad. He had issues with alcohol and some drugs but nothing that seemed to control his body. Anger controlled Lenord. But treated with respect and left alone to think on his own, he started to smile and became one of the happier men in the ward.

Charlie*:* Charlie, whom I liked the most, had tried kill himself when the depression got too much. Unfortunately, by accident, he attempted the event on his son's birthday and failed. Thus, the guilt only increased the problem.

Ken and Kyle: Ken and Kyle, fifty and twenty-three, respectively, were high suicide potential. Ken had tried three times and Kyle, once. I feel Ken will not stop. Kyle had a three-month-old baby, and he was fighting to make a better life. The doctors were very serious about Kyle's next steps. They wanted him to demonstrate that he knew what to do and show cognitive organizational skills for the future. While Kyle and I were talking, I told him he needed to outline the goals and put them in a timeline.

The next day Kyle was at the main table working away. At the end of it all, he created an old proposal format I told him about. Kyle saved his life in the institutional system by redirecting the doctors.

Kyle had laid out his goals, the actions plan to make it happen, and what he expected. Kyle did it all, successfully.

Steve: Steve is a unique kind of man. Steve was disliked by everyone and he was ready to explode. Steve was an intelligent lawyer from Cape Cod but a blatant racist. On the tenth day, Steve threw chairs down the hall and hit whatever he could. It is a credit to the staff--they relaxed him. Later that day, Steve was moved to a ward for more violent psychiatric patients.

Ellen: Ellen was a religious zealot who arrived on the ninth day. She would carry the cross around the ward and repeat scripture. She would do this often and loudly.

Ellen would get in individuals' faces and start screaming. By the eleventh day, I realized she liked classical music and dance. I suggested to the floor manager, Ginger, to allow her the privilege of using the educational room as her music and dance room. Ginger and the staff took my advice, and all was quiet for an hour at a time, day after day. For coming up with the idea, Dave, Lenord, Charlie and I were granted extra TV bowling, billiards, and Frisbee time.

Paul: Paul joined the happy guys and gals group which allowed everyone safety from other patients and staff. Paul was six-foot-tall, around twenty-five years old, and green eyed, red-haired boy who got into heroin after high school. As with Lenord, you did not want to set this man off.

Once I got to know the ward patients, the reason I committed myself became buried. One good thing came to light very fast; the isolation kept all the negative environmental stimuli outside the ward. You had to exist in a closed world controlled by staff. I was becoming institutionalized.

Let me return to Paul. During one of his girlfriend's visits, she dropped two twenty-dollar bills on the floor and then went through the locked door. I had picked up the bills, knowing it had to belong to a visitor due to the location. She quickly returned, crying. I walked up and asked her and the nurse what the problem was? Vicki said she lost all the money she had for food! I asked how much? Once she said two twenty-dollar bills, I pulled the money out of my pocket and returned it to her. Her feeling of relief and happiness was overwhelming, but nothing compared to the shock on the others' faces--honestly! Dollars in a ward were like gold since all money was confiscated when we were admitted. Paul became a Brian Masters fan!

The staff: The system breaks the staff into groups. There are the doctors, psychiatrists, mental health and medical staff. Supporting them is the head nurse (nurse in charge), associate nurses, and staff. Doctors, psychiatrists, and mental health staff are normally on call. The staff is divided into day and night and their work hours are based on the budget that the hospital can afford.

The Head Nurse. Mary was the head nurse. The patients quickly understood who oversaw the ward. Once a rule was broken or you stepped out of line, Mary's quick tongue or sarcasm would cut you out of the herd. For example, Mary had the authority to remove your ability to go to the cafeteria; eating a prepared plate alone became an isolation cell in itself--a sad isolation.

The Associate Nurse and Staff. These staff people had their own tasks and they reported to Mary. As in any closed society, people assume their role based on their personalities. The nurses and staff watched all the patients, yet there were those who bent the rules and those who did not. Power was at top of the food chain. As a patient, you learned to compliment power and praise it; then a patient and his group could play.

The Med Nurse. This was a role I knew nothing about. Three times a day, the patients were given their required medication from behind the half door or screen. My pills were your standard older man pills except for the sleeping pills. I would not realize until six months later that the substance abuse patients need an imitation high drug to sustain. You could see the "Pavlov's dog" behavior of the patients as the clock approached medication delivery time.

Should you follow a path of drug use and be admitted to a hospital, it is a fact that you will end up at the med door. Should you be fortunate to read this book prior to any institutionalization, get "One Flew Over the Cuckoo Nest." We were in it and Nurse Mary was Nurse Ratchet.

Floor and wing layout: At least at this facility floors were assigned according to your behavior and the severity of your illness. The first floor was for people who, at first evaluation, were non-aggressive or had limited mental illness. The second floor had those who attempted suicide, overdosed, or were admitted by family members who had reached their limits.

The second floor was for people beyond rational and reasonable understanding of who they are, what they did, or what they are doing. Discipline was far more severe and positive reinforcement did not seem to work. Code Blue is an intercom alert to the staff that violence is taking place. Most of the time it was on the second floor. When a code blue is called staff members on that floor drop everything, code the locked doors, and run to the problem.

The wings are divided into east and west. The west wing was for individuals below the age of seventeen. The east wing was for ages eighteen and above.

Cafeteria: The cafeteria had outstanding food. That is why losing the privilege to choose your food and eat with other patients was truly a weapon. I believe it was designed that way.

Seating in the cafeteria was determined by floor and category of patients. Our floor on the east wing would eat after the mentally impaired but before the more violent. We came to eat when called so as not to, even potentially, get in the cross hairs of a very pissed-off patient from another floor.

> Due to an issue on the second floor, the intensive patients had to eat at the same time as our ward. Simply due to an exchange of words about a rock band name on a tie-dyed shirt, a very mad twenty-seven-year-old man tore into another patient. The staff and guards were right there, and I did nothing to help; it's best to just stay out to the way.

It was at this point I realized that I had to work with the system or be back on the street. It is interesting how an *"acceptable worldwide addiction"*, smoking, becomes a form of money when you're not free to get cigarettes. I do not smoke so my allocation from the staff went to whomever I felt was a good person. As the days went by, I used behavior modification to dole out my cigs. The people I hung with got my cigs.

I was adjusting to the system to survive to the next steps. But what were the next steps? No one was addressing the issues I laid out.

The Treatment

I can break my treatment into classes and doctor consultations.

Classes: The classes were run by social workers with specialized areas of expertise. One class might be anti-aggression, another might be discussions of personal positive points, another dealing with substance abuse problems, but most were games. Games were to help improve your memory and attention span. I quickly understood the more classes you attended, the higher the patient approval score by the medical staff. Play the game and get a free pass.

Doctor meetings: These meetings had substance. I was very focused on learning and self-improvement. Once the doctor realized I was serious, the mental health staff for outside assistance kicked in. My plan was simple:

- Secure housing

- Social Services to address substance abuse

- Get my car back

- Start using the web for find and apply for six figure jobs

- Get an hourly job to sustain car loan, cell, and food

- Build back up and move back to the Boros (Boston suburbs)

The doctor and staff took it upon themselves to secure the housing and therapy services. I was even granted the privilege of having phone interviews in the staff room.

Institutionalized, patients torment patients:

> Lenord had been begging his mother to take him back to their house. He promised anything if she would agree. One morning, Lenord's mother agreed, and she showed up at the hospital to speak with the doctors. Do you remember Ellen, the religious zealot who would get into people's faces? Well, Ellen knew Lenord was going to leave that day *if he behaved.* So, Ellen lit into Lenord with every name in the book, anti-Christian comments and the "n word" at the exact same time his mother was signing the release forms. Lenord

lost control. I was standing *right behind him*, feeling the intensity coming from his body and watching his movements. Ryan, the staff guard was *more than three steps* away. As Lenord lunged at Ellen, I locked both of his arms behind him and stepped on the back of his feet. That gave everyone time to circle Lenord and calm him down. Ryan, the staff guard, said nothing, the Med Nurse behind the half door said nothing, and Lenord's mother, who was at the other end of the ward, signed the papers. Leonord said, "Thank you, Brian." I said, "Just do what your mother says." He smiled, shook my hand, and he was on his way home. I know in my heart, Lenord, if he wanted to, could have broken my arm lock.

Pembrook Comes to an End

On the eleventh day of my stay, I was informed by the doctor that I would be released the following Monday. Mental Health had secured a bed in a dry house in Jamaica Plain for me. I would be having daily classes in a nearby town from 8 to 3 and then taken by bus back to the dry house. I told Mike of the move and asked him to hold tight to the car and other items that could be useful at the dry house. Mike went on to preach at me that being out of the hospital does not mean going back to the old ways; I embraced his speech wholeheartedly.

The night before, Charlie had gone into deep depression and was not capable of coming out of his room to sit. The next morning, while we were lining up at the cafeteria door, my roommate Tom walked up to me. Tom shook my hand and said he would have never made it this far had I not been there. I felt weak at the knees and was speechless for a change. Later, I felt odd when I thought maybe this could be why I went through all these experiences, to help someone.

60

In the office, I was given my bags of clothes, my cell, charger, and my discharge papers. Everyone shook hands, and I was told to go the main entrance for my ride to Jamaica Plain. Just before they them unlocked the door, I walked over to Charlie's room to say good bye and good luck. I knocked and look through the window. Charlie was curled up in the fetal position and unresponsive to the knock. Charlie was depressed, sedated, and out of it. I felt like he had lost something. I never saw Charlie again.

I literally jumped into the taxi and road north toward Boston.

Let's look at my institutionalization and the events to follow as learning experiences. It is a must that you understand the people and events to come are instrumental in mistakes that are made by me and others. This is the start of what can be defined as the "Street Culture" or "Subculture." The term Subculture is not meant to be a negative stigma but is a real description of people on the street and their attempts at survival.

This section of the book is the reality of addiction. It is a snapshot of what can be, which is the reason I am drawing from the journals I kept during that time. I want you to have the benefit of knowing before it happens to you, your family, or your friends. Maybe this book is a confirmation of what you have been though. Maybe it is a confirmation of what you are experiencing now. Maybe you can visualize these experiences and be motivated to find a path out.

I have described the institutionalization hierarchy, the facility, and patients in detail. I did this because as we move on, when I revisit a hospital almost all procedures and staff assignments are the same. The personalities and facility may change, but the hierarchy and treatments are similar. The question is whether the outcome is different.

The point is, had I addressed the three reasons I committed myself? After two weeks of state paid health care, the answer was "no." I will do the best I can to translate the hell and the reasons for failures and success.

The Housing

It felt like my first day at high school or college; I had no idea what to expect. All I knew is that one of the doctors had listened to me and put the wheels in motion for "understanding why I was drinking, my depression, and changing it." One thing was for sure, this step was not institutionalization. I was no longer restricted to times, types of food, language, appearance, smell, love/hate behavior, and times for sleeping.

The First Dry House Combined with Institutional Education

Sizing me up: I was driven to the house at 750 Darren Street in Jamaica Plain. My mind and eyes were clear, my body was steady, and I was focused. The neighborhood was mixed with all cultures and colors, reminding me of the neighborhood I grew up in back in Syracuse, New York. Instinctively, I knew how to behave.

The house was an old New England triple-decker with an iron fence around the property. No one could go through the front gate unless you lived or worked there. Knowing I was meeting the decision maker of the house, I wore khaki pants, docksiders, and a nice shirt. From the gate, I was led into the house and the large office on the right. The office once had been library or sitting room when it was first built. Kelly Thomas asked me to sit down while he reviewed my discharge papers from the hospital. Kelly was approximately 5'9'', light complexion, red hair, wearing jeans and a shirt. Kelly had been there and come back, as you might say.

Due to my attitude, speech, and dress, Kelly said he would put me on the second floor with Ryan. The second floor was reserved for serious individuals who wanted sobriety, to be clean, and find a way out. The third floor had rooms for three to four men, off the street or the hospital, had the same desire of being straight but more likely to relapse. The first floor was reserved for long timers who paid for their rooms and had been straight for a good amount of time.

To be straightforward, I was a pompous ass. I felt I deserved the second floor because this was a temporary stop back to my old life. Sure, I would dedicate myself to learning and working, but in my mind, this was my last stop in housing. Especially now that I had money in the bank. I even paid extra to have a spot for my car in the gated parking lot.

Mike Garrison drove in from the suburbs to pick me up and take me back to get my car and clothes. The car had been at the Garrisons' since Mike had paid to get it out of the tow yard. When I stayed at the hospital, I had sold items to pay my tickets, registration, and insurance; now I could drive. I loaded the car with my broken laptop and screen, one full dress suit, shoes, everyday clothes, and personal items.

Bedrooms: My room was a two bedroom, which had two dressers, a TV, and two closets. I quickly sorted the clothes and set up the laptop and its attached monitor, so the internet house key would connect me to the outside world. Ryan came into to the room from his retail job blocks away. Ryan was 5'5", white with black hair, and around 23 years old. Ryan had a speech impediment, which was one of the reasons he kept to himself, did not laugh, and played videos on his fully functional laptop. I found out a week later, Ryan was depressed, shunned by his family, and had come off heroin.

Chores: I was the new guy, so my chore was to clean the full bathroom thoroughly. All chemicals, sponges, mops, and gloves were stored in the pantry.

State mandated requirements: Every other week there would be a knock on the door for a piss line up. No exceptions. If you refused or tested positive, you had to pack your clothes and you would be escorted out to the street. Every week, all house members were required to attend an AA meeting in the old library. The two full weeks I was there, I always ended up sitting next to a guy who smelled like whiskey.

When you have been sober for a period of time, your senses can pick up any alcohol or pot smell. Again, I felt better than them; I was not drinking, and I was holding tough.

People: I knew that my dry housemates were there due to alcohol, pot, cocaine, crack, opiates, heroin, or all the above. It was at this stage I learned that you ask no questions. Thank God, I learned it here. Anywhere else, stupid questions got you shunned, punched, or singled out as law enforcement. In other words, this house was mild and at the top of the food chain of housing. This is the place you want to be. *I had no clue.*

Kit: Kit had been a teacher in Braintree. He was white, five feet tall at best, and forty-two years old. Alcohol and pot had caught up with him. He lived on the second floor and was happy to be there.

Michael: Michael was on the third floor, and we hit it off from the start. Michael was black, 5'9", well-built, bald, and wore a bandana. Maybe it was because of my training with all colors and backgrounds in martial arts, but Mike and I knew when to laugh, smile, give space, and not ask questions.

Ryan: Unfortunately for Ryan, after I left someone from the third floor jimmied the room door and took his laptop. The laptop was Ryan's escape and lifeline. A person on the third floor who needed money for drugs had singled him out. I heard Ryan lost it.

Larry: Larry was a great guy who knew his shit. Larry had been a top chef on Martha's Vineyard during the seventies and eighties. Larry would use his money or state funds and cookay up a huge quantity of chicken, meat, or fish.

Kyle: A short guy who was never seen much. I can give you no description. My only interaction was knocking on his door twice. One for the piss test and the other was to tell him the manager needed to talk to him. He had been there for a time, was trusted, and you never came into his space.

Institutional Education

Education at the Davis Support Group: July 15, 2014 started with the evaluation of my history, the classes that I would take, and the type of people I would be grouped with. All the instructors and directors held doctorates in substance use. Now we were getting somewhere at addressing why I came. It was night and day from the hospital.

There were three directors assigned to roughly thirty-five men and woman. The men and women were there because they had legal requirements, committed themselves, or were committed by their family. My director was Dr. John, and we got right into depression and its partnership with substances.

My goals were outlined and then would be monitored by Dr. John and me.

Therapy:

- Two weeks understanding of personal issues

- AA arrangements

- Physical and mental health plan

Personal Rebuild:

- Housing

- Part time jobs

- Long term, high paying job

- Repayment of outstanding debts

- Budget for cash flow and paying bills

- Move from the Boston area within the 128 belt, back to the suburbs.

Classes: The topic of many classes was the brain and its control of reasoning, actions leading to results, and understanding the "why" of behavior. This I fully understood and embraced. First, we started with the parts of the brain and their function. This led to discussions on genetic influences as compared to environmental influences. Then we would go into situations, thinking, reasoning, options to take, and consequences. Each day was something different or built on what other instructors had taught before. These professionals had it down and I looked forward to each new day.

One lesson that stood out was the Yale Medical School discovery of the two sections of the brain that split behavior--rational behavior in the prefrontal cortex and primitive behavior in the limbic part of the brain. The latter is the human survival and pressure control. The PFC controls the urges and the logic of the behavior. Should the two be disconnected, then control can be lost, and pleasure stimuli will take over. Simple but true. This was something that made sense to me--but how to stop the disconnect?

*This is the scientific approach to understanding what is happening to you. By understanding the **triggers**, genetic influences, friends and family and resources which affect an individual, you have a greater chance at controlling destructive behavior. One thing for sure, the program that I signed up for was at the top of the health system. Unfortunately, **knowing** is not **doing**.*

By the end of the 1ˢᵗ week, I was 3 weeks sober. My head was clear and my motivation was back.

My first practical lesson learned: The bus would take us back to the house at 2:30 pm on the dot. The point behind the release time was for everyone to get back to their homes in different cities and beat the rush hour. It also gave us time to get to jobs or achieve other goals on our lists.

I was attempting to tackle both the short term and long-term job search simultaneously. Since my head was clear and my speech was intact, I arranged a phone interview with startup tech company out of California and a face-to-face interview at a nearby convenience store. During my first weekend at the dry house, I walked to nearby retail companies looking for part-time jobs. I was confident that all my work and learning would come together quickly. My brain would be repaired, reasoning would be intact, and social drinking could return.

> By the middle of the first week, it was obvious that the staff of the therapy facility used hand sanitizer dispensers mounted on the walls. One morning, one of the doctors stood up front of the class and started to breathe in heavily. I had nicknamed him Sam Kenison, Ph.D. due to his unusual behavior in front of the people and the way he proved a relevant point. This time, he had a serious look on his face and his arms were crossed over his chest. He looked over to the person in the chair to his right and asked, "Have you been drinking!" The answer to the question was "No." She said, "I just came in, cleaned up, and sat down." Then a look of relief and disgust was on his face. "I cannot believe they cannot make a disinfectant that does not smell like Vodka! Here we are teaching triggers and yet what we have our

hands smells like alcohol?" Everyone laughed, and we opened a short discussion. *That is when it hit me between the eyes.* The Google Express Manager in LA thought he smelled vodka on me during the last test deliveries. It was hand sanitizer. All I could do was log it in my memory and shake my head. Then I started laughing; the shirt I was wearing was a Google Express golf shirt given to me at the training in California. Ironic, but not funny.

My self-imposed financial support plan: When I had accepted the generosity of Mike Garrison to get my car out of hock and pay my ticket, I knew something had to be done to pay my bills before I found work. The fact was that I had destroyed most of the trust I had with family, friends, and business partners. How would I continue to get financial help?

That is when I asked Mike to control all my bank accounts. I would pay the bills that were important, and Mike would watch every transaction. *I created a self-imposed financial trust.* It was my job to call every one of my support group and explain the plan. Any money provided to help my goal would not go to substance use. The plan worked, and my support family embraced my serious intent.

That is when Martin Phillips came into the picture. Martin had provided me with $1,000 to replant myself in Hollywood with Johnny and he had witnessed that failure. Martin was my mentor at Xerox Corporation, where I had worked in the 70's and 80's. Martin seemed to understand. We had both built successful leasing organizations and made large amounts of money. Martin took it upon himself to recruit financial aid from our old business friends, most of whom understood my plight because their own life experiences.

Now I had some help.

You may have had to live with a friend or family member and pay for their help with your food stamps. If you lacked the financial support I had, your downward spiral into the street culture of addiction could be faster than mine due to the lack of that important support--money.

Episodes at the MassHealth backed Davis Group: *My classes at The Davis Group, which were funded by MassHealth, were a very positive experience, but those educational classes had rules and are not intended for everyone. Here are a few examples of what I mean.*

> **The Newbury Street man:** The Newbury Street Man was at just one of the classes. Because the attendees in the classes changed almost daily, it was routine to go around the room and have new people introduce themselves. The format was to ask why they were here, what they did the night before, and their thoughts. The Newbury man was white, about 5'11", good looking, and dressed like the performer Prince. He said he was at the classes because he was losing control and needed to either stop drinking or find an answer. He told his story about being at a respectable level in the fashion industry and he was living on Newbury Street. Part of the fashion industry culture is to attend parties, *like the party he attended the night before,* where he had three martinis. He knew he may have a problem and that is why he was here. After the first break, and without any explanation, the Newbury Street Man's seat was empty.

It was not until two years later that I would learn the alcohol content in your body is higher the day after a binge than when you stopped and slept the night before. The Davis Group director had given him a breath test and he failed.

The woman who would not speak: This woman was admitted to the program but refused to engage in any conversation or class discussions. She was there for three days and then left. This was how I learned from the staff that all lunch food was counted and tagged because it was free and valuable on the street. This was my first introduction to taking food back out on the street to sell or to eat. The woman took her food and anyone else's she could walk out with.

The Plan is Working

By the beginning of the second week, July 20th, my plan was coming together. Stop and Shop might hire me. A Chicago company wanted a second interview. I called Johnny with the good news, but he was playing golf.

Doctors who kill: On July 22, I went to class and then drove Guillerio, at member of the house, to his primary doctor at a neighborhood practice. It was at that appointment I made a *medical* mistake and had my *first street culture healthcare realization.*

The waiting room at the doctor's office was packed with people from the ages of nineteen on up-- mostly young people. Guillerio was twenty-five, a great guy, and very sincere about improving himself. The appointments were running an hour to an hour and a half late, *but no one cared.* The conversations in the waiting room gave me a life of learning. Each girl and guy struck up conversations on the drugs they were getting prescribed or what they needed next. Unfortunately, I had no clue what they were talking about, but Guillerio did. It was the first time I had heard of Oxycodone, Percocet, or crystal meth.

While Guillerio was with his doctor, I struck up a conversation with the receptionist and explained my situation. The receptionist brought out a nurse who explained the doctor's practice as a local primary care. At this point, I considered switching to this doctor who was closer to Jamaica Plain, and knew the Boston area system and the local therapists. I filled out the forms to switch doctors and indicate where my meds should be sent.

During the ride back to the dry house, Guillerio tried to reinforce my decision to switch to his doctor. I asked him why. Guillerio's answer was, "because you can get what you want, in any quantity, when you want it!"

This was my first introduction to a lifestyle totally foreign to me. I would realize later that this was the health system, the politicians, drug companies, and doctors' pill factory system. It would not be until 2016 that New Hampshire and national statistics on opioid abuse made an impact. If people were not dying at such a high rate, it would still be going on.

The street is the street: Dr. John, the director of the therapy told me to go the SMAK organization in one of the nearby towns and apply for housing. He suggested either a room in a *dry house* or a room in *alternative housing*. I still had no clue what that meant.

The way my first dry house was run is a credit to the system. Managers, who were part owners, did not take any shit. Everyone knew where they stood and what was expected. But the street is the street.

Around, July 21st, Michael asked if I had five dollars he could have for a day. I knew that the five dollars was expendable, and I may never see it again, but I gave it to him. He mentioned that he was waiting for a ride and unfortunately a dude down the street may be stiffing him for hundreds of dollars.

Michael kept eyeing a three-decker house down the street. Then a yellow cobra pulled up and Michael got in. Later that evening I saw Michael in the hallway and he gave me my five dollars back, with a smile. I had seen that face and smile before. We were solid. The next morning, Michael was gone. I asked Larry what was up with Michael? Larry's response was short and sweet. "Brian, he took everything he had in the house and just left in the middle of the night." There was that moment of silence where you ask no questions unless more information is given. Larry looked down the street and said, "He got back what someone tried to fuck him out of, that maybe it?" I would meet Michael again, shortly.

It became apparent to me that even though this was the top of the line in health care housing, you either recovered and went back to where you were, you adapted and stayed, or you failed and moved on. *The more I learned, the more my feeling of enthusiasm and positive energy started to wane. I wanted so much to be back in the space of pre-2007.*

Days of Days Past – a Trigger

Triggers: Jeff Lent, the business friend who let me stay at his house while he was in France, sent Mike $500 under the new rules of my support plan. Now that there were some funds, I drove to a nearby town and spent the day with Mike. We reviewed what my car needed and drove to the CarMax retail store.

It was at that store I realized what the doctor at the Davis Group meant by triggers. As Mike and I walked in the door, staring me straight in the face was a life-sized poster of a tan Yamaha, three-passenger jet ski. The doctors are correct! Triggers can be dangerous and this one put my body into total dread. As Mike walked the aisles, I stared at that poster vividly recalling the two identical jet skis I bought for my family for our lake house. Our house on the water looked directly south for twenty-five miles of water and mountains. I could feel the ride, hear the laughs, and see the smiles on my son and his friends. I never said a word to Mike and Liz, but there it was, a painful emotion, a feeling of regret. *I had to mask the pain*. Now I realized the importance of the reverse trigger, taught by the Davis Group program.

My journal, that day says, "I broke the code." I can rightly say that I cannot remember, but I assume I drank at Mike's house on the way to the dry house. Triggers create that feeling: "I want to be in control like before and live that fun over again!" The impulse is an overwhelming emotion where logical decision-making is overwhelmed by the irrational need, want, and desire.

The fall from the plan: By the end of week, job interviews were starting to stall, and the classes were coming to an end. Mike had left for an out-of-state meeting and Liz was without a car. Liz and I had known each other since 1978 and we had a true friendship. Since I had free time, Liz and I made plans to go to the Commons in Boston for sightseeing and arts shows.

Now I was in my comfort zone. I was **complacent** and excited about being back to where I wanted to be and should be.

I went to a nearby store and bought vodka for the outing. Unfortunately, my body and my mind were not accepting any substance. Once I arrived at Liz's, I was over the limit and I fell asleep at Mike's house. I realized my four weeks of sobriety had been broken and the guilt became overwhelming.

It was my bad luck to meet with Kelley Thomas, the manager of the dry house because I was out overnight and missing in action. The bottle fell out of the backpack. My stay there ended. Larry gathered some of my clothes for me and asked me to leave. The remaining personal items would be given to me when I returned in two days.

I slept in the car.

The last day at therapy at the Davis Group: I decided to suck in my pride and go back for the last day of class. The system was efficient enough to let the director know of my dismissal from the dry house. Dr. John had a surprised look on his face which indicated that he knew. I said, "You heard what happened?" Dr. John, said, "Yes, but no one has ever come back!" At that point, we started to work on next steps, and I attended the last morning class.

John provided me with a list of shelters, which, if they had an open bed, would take me for a night, maybe longer. Because my plan was to move west, back to the Boros, I called a facility in one of the towns I wanted to live in. The manager told me it was first come, first served, and his facility was a dry shelter. What did that mean?

I want to remind you what this book is about. What it is and what it is not! This book might allow you to see the reality of what can await anyone, in any city, and in any country. It is not about me or my stupidity to drink. It is about the world you will enter if you don't address your addiction early. The people, their language, their smell, their abuse, their hunger and the abuse of themselves. It is about their breaks in life or the bad breaks in life. **Hope leads to Will, Will leads to Planning, Planning leads to Actions, and Actions lead to Success.**

I had committed myself to a hospital for three specific reasons. Were any of the reasons addressed? Did anyone explain the places and their purpose? The first step after institutionalization was a dry house combined with relevant classes; it taught physical and mental repair, yet I had no preparation for the outside challenges yet to come.

Follow my actions so you can walk in my shoes or the shoes of others that I met. Do not cloud your thoughts and say how stupid that action could be. Refocus to what was around me, my struggle against the stigma of addiction, and the realization of what works through trial and error.

Shelters – Enter Hell with Eyes Wide Open

The First Dry Shelter and the Street

I drove directly to the Waltham shelter using my GPS. I parked the car on the street and made my way up a flight to stairs passing women and men who were smoking, talking, and looking at my clothes.

I met the managers who seemed sympathetic about substance use and mental health. Both Julio and Guy read me the rules and assigned me bed 33. They made a copy of my MassHealth card, driver's license, and *gave me a sobriety test* using a color stick.

There were two bedrooms, two bathrooms, a kitchen, a den and the manager's office. The kitchen had one small TV, a small microwave, coffee pots, small lockers, and a table. The main den had two couches and a TV; the den was converted into a bedroom after 8 pm. The main bedroom had roughly twenty-five bunk beds and fifty beds.

The one large bathroom had two showers, two sinks, and two urinals. The small bathroom had one toilet and one shower; this bathroom was reserved for the female staff manager during her day shift.

Now that I have arrived at the shelters, I will describe the people I met there. To shelter management, you are a number associated with the bed. The people are like shadows moving in and out of the building. Food, money, cigarettes, and drugs are valuables.

Rules: All tenants needed to attempt good hygiene. No smoking was allowed inside the building, only on the porch or near the entrance. Lights were turned out at ten pm and everyone had to be in bed. Each person oversaw placing his paper bags, backpacks, and carry bags, under, in front, in back, or on the bed. Anything in the walk way was fair game for the shelter staff or tenants. I tied my carry bag to my foot.

The Lawrence Street shelter was a dry shelter, which means no alcohol or drugs can be detected. Should there be any doubt about someone's behavior, management had the right to test him and make him leave. In other words, *your insurance is shut off.* All tenants had to be out of the building by eight am, and we could return at four-thirty pm.

Chores: The chores would change with the demands of the managers. While I was there I cleaned the toilets, showers, or mopped the floors. I was paying my dues, kneeling down and scrubbing toilets used by 60+ other men; the showers were no better.

The streets: By eight am, we would have had to make our beds and have the bathrooms cleaned. Then we had to fend for themselves. The sixty-five men scattered to

- The town library

- The parks

- Businesses looking for work

- Their jobs

- The streets to discuss what is free and get and use the substance of choice

- The churches, food pantries, lunch and dinner gathering places for the homeless

I created a pattern around the library, food kitchens, and interviews. My advantage was that I had the car and the suitcases inside it. Julio, the manager, told me of the garage across the street. If you parked in one particular area and obeyed the signs, the police and parking management would look the other way. But if your vehicle was broken into, you were on your own.

Street kindness: Unknown to me at the time, this would be my home from July 26th to August 19th. In the shelter, color, race, and background *could matter*, and what you do and say is important. For example, the man in the bunk next to mine had been in the town for years. It was accepted behavior for him to hold and sleep with his stuffed dog. He would carry the dog in his pack or put it on his bed for when he returned. One evening, his stuffed dog came up missing and the man started losing his mind. He was shaking, yelling, and crying. Love for the dog had kept this man stable. It was then that I discovered the hierarchy of the tenants in the shelters. Certain individuals with tenure and violent intentions let it be known that they made the rules. Return the stuffed dog or suffer the consequences. The dog, miraculously, showed up in the corner of the room. The joke was over, and you could hear the man crying with happiness as he spoke kind words to his dog.

Food: Other than shelter, food was the next requirement for survival. I have seen so many men and women just let themselves go thin, pale, and weak by not taking the time to eat. The local Catholic church would have a dinner for us every night except weekends and holidays. If you would like a hot meal cooked by a group who wanted to help the homeless, you sat, waited and behaved. At six pm, on the dot, the Father would appear and preach the sermon for the night. If you were smart, you shut up and listened. The tables attracted similar people. Families would gather at one table, battered women and hookers at another, and the men of the shelter and the locals at yet another. Women and children were served first and then the men. Rarely were there seconds.

> While standing in line I looked up from my food to see Julie Taylor, one of the executives of a midsize company to which I had sold computers, now serving from the ovens. In my past life I had been an up-and-coming IBM AS/400 salesman who was on the board of the IBM New England User Group. Here I was face-to-face with my past. She was helping, and I was the one being helped.

Michael comes back: After finishing my chores at the shelter, I would rest in the TV room if a space on the couch were available. I kept my head low and presented a low profile. I sat, put my cell phone between my legs, and looked at the man next to me. *It was Michael.* The headband was gone, and hair was growing, but it was Michael. We said nothing to each other. When you are there, your past is gone. I felt bad because he looked weaker than in the Jamaica Plain dry house; little did I know, so did I.

The raw truth: Depending on the day or night a shelter varies. The first shelter experience included:

• Men in old ripped clothes

• The smell of piss and shit from the bathroom

• Old timers and newbies watching you and your moves

Threats, theft, and drug detox are the norm. One night a twenty-two-year-old was taken away for bouncing off the walls, and another night wallets were stolen, including mine. The reality is, "you leave me alone and I will leave you alone." Yet, there was also kindness and the desire to help. We were in a brotherhood, frequently trading clothes, shoes, and bags. Loaning cigs was a ritual. Sometimes food, drugs, and alcohol were shared.

> Days after I arrived, two new tenants were accepted into the shelter. They were from west of Springfield, looking to get to the City of Boston and its streets and lifestyle. The two had no hesitation to speak, talk about themselves, and asked tenants to advise them where to go in Boston. Julio had put them in separate rooms because it was apparent that they were a gay couple. One night, Michael turned to me and spoke for the first time. He said, "They will not last." I answered, "Two days at the most." The long- timers reminded me of the character Archie Bucker; they wanted nothing to do with these young men even though they were pleasant and harmless. These two visitors were forced to experience what I can only describe as hate in the air. _This was a life style stigma_. They were gone in two days.

I become the target: My interview at the convenience story and my job search at the library were paying off; I had a job and a start date. Along with my new-found confidence, I became more complacent at the shelter. I started to be myself and made people smile and laugh. My background showed, and the long-time locals did not like it. At the church dinner, I realized I was being shunned. On August 18th, my wallet was stolen while I slept. I had tied my carry bag to my foot, but I felt nothing in the night.

The next day I met an old friend for drinks to discuss a potential sales position. I let my guard down by acting as if I were back in my old business days. When I drove back, I entered the kitchen at the shelter, still dressed like a professional. I announced that I had been robbed, and I needed the contents back. Two old-timers left the room and ten minutes later Julio asked to see me. I was tested for alcohol and to Julio's dismay the test turned a very light color. The two men had smelled the alcohol and turned me in. I had to leave.

Are you seeing the common denominator here? Every time you let your guard down and you use any substance, something bad happens. Whether you mess up or someone wants to mess with you, you lose. Those who let their guard down are at risk from those who see you differently, as a threat, or an object of hate. Michael had said as much two weeks before when he left for his next adventure. Now I had to explain this to the Garrisons, my friends, and my family without losing face. I was out in the street without a license, identification, or the pictures of Johnny that kept me going. But I had learned a lot.

Back to the Street

Living in the car and the woods: I was on my own, and I could not bring myself to call anyone for assistance. This was my problem, and I needed to address it myself. Now the car was my primary home.

The safest place to sleep at night was the parking lot of large apartment complexes. As I had done before, I would park away from the light poles and as least two rows from any cars on either side. That way, I could block the light coming in and I could roll the windows down without being seen. Cleaning up at the fast food restaurants was a standard procedure. At one of the restaurants I had a conversation with a man who informed me that sleeping in your car is illegal depending on the town enforcing it. Even if it were not true, I decided not to be caught. The next few nights I would park the car in a location with woods nearby, take my old clothes out of the car, and use them as a mattress. It worked.

The car breaks down: One evening I had traveled to Ashland to rotate the areas where I spent the night. I parked in a grocery store parking lot to relax. Lori, the librarian I had dated, lived in Ashland.

Drive just half a mile down Route 126, take a left at the light, and four condos on the left were all the comforts of home. Though I needed help badly, I could not bring myself to call Lori who had begged me to stay in New England and then left me hanging just a year before. I got pissed and attempted to start the car and move on, but the car was dead. I opened the hood and saw corrosion over the battery cables. When I reached to close the hood, I cut my finger slightly. This might seem minor to most people, but ever since the 2011 operation and the infection, any cut would make me bleed without stopping. I walked to the fields next to the miniature golf course where Lori and I had played. I made a spot on the ground to sleep. My finger bled until it finally stopped. In the morning, when the strip mall stores opened, I called Triple A and had the car fixed. I was burnt out, bloody, smelled like dirty grass, and glassy eyed from the small bottle I bought.

I begged for help: I could not take it anymore. I drove to Framingham to the headquarters of SMAK, a non-profit funded by the state to provide housing and other resources. I walked to the front desk. Short and sweet I said, "I am done sleeping in my car. I need a place to live so I can work and get my feet on the ground." Just by looking at me, they knew the seriousness of my plight. Three hours later, I had a room at the Palladin house on Linesman Street; a sober house in Marlborough.

It was September 4ᵗʰ, 2014 and all this had happened in just three months. I had achieved some of my goals: an hourly job, a roof over my head, and I was back in the Boros.

*While I was waiting for help, there was another person in the lobby. He was a young adult in his mid-twenties with a long goatee, tattoos, the shakes, and glazed eyes. **I had no idea this young man would severely impact my life. So much for the negative.***

The Second Dry Shelter

The shelter: As I was driving up Rt. 85 from Framingham, I started to relax and feel positive. Now I was in the MetroWest area, which is entirely different from the towns and cities within the 128 belt around Boston. At least, that is what I thought.

I pulled into the city, recognizing the street and main highways that ran through it. My memories of this town included buying hockey equipment for Johnny, business meetings at restaurants, and sales calls at corporations. I immediately performed "reverse triggers" to limit those memories. Now I was going to live here. I pulled up and I saw a sign on a building reading Transitional Housing. I parked the car and walked to the front door. The door was locked and could only be unlocked by an individual looking at a mirror positioned on the building to monitor the door. I stood there, heard a buzz, and I opened the door.

The shelter was one floor with three bunk-bed rooms, one kitchen, two bathrooms, the manager's office and a mop closet.

The procedures were very like the previous house and shelter. The intake manager reviewed the rules, took my prescription drugs, and showed me to my bed. Tenants were assigned chores every week if they intended on staying more than a day. The rules were strict and had to be obeyed: follow the curfew hours, stay clean and sober, and no fighting or swearing. If you break the rules, you might get one warning then you could lose your bed.

I have described people at the hospital, the dry house, and the first shelter. Now I will detail the individuals at this second shelter. This is the learning experience of the good and bad on the street. It may even allow you to see yourself; how would you react to some the circumstances?

The people:

Tim P.: Tim was fifty-four years old, approximately 5'10", and needed dental work. Tim had a friendly personality, plenty of common sense, read constantly, and had lived in the local area when he was sober. Tim was a skilled mechanic who lost all his tools due to a divorce. Tim's problem was alcohol.

Andy P.: (Tim's son): Tim's son worked at one of the leading grocery store chains in the area. I know that his father's influence prevented him from substance use. Andy mentally functioned at the age of a sixteen-year-old. I would reconnect with Tim and Andy at an extended-stay hotel in late spring of 2015.

Carlos: Carlos was a carpenter from Cuba, approximately 5'4", and quick with a smile. Alcohol was Carlos's addiction, and it kept him living pay check to pay check. We became good friends. Carlos wanted me to succeed to prove that it could be done. Carlos would make me dinner five out of seven nights, so I could maintain the pace I needed to get out of the house.

Adam: Adam had no occupation that I knew of. He came from an influential family. His hair was long and over his eyes. He shuffled, walked with his face down, and said nothing. He had a brand new 2014 car he would use to sleep during the day. Adam would occasionally shower and shave. He would perform his house chores and obey the house curfew just enough to have a roof over his head. Adam was scary.

Ruff: Ruff was a large, well-built gentleman. He was roughly six feet tall, had had an addictive disease, spent time in jail, and had found religion. Ruff and I went face-to-face one night, but we both realized it was a stupid thing to do. We apologized to each other and became good friends. Ruff knew far more about the street than I did, and he taught me not be disruptive.

The bad seeds:

Lu: Lu was the young man I had seen in the SMAK waiting room. Lu was a white man in his twenties, about 6'2", thin, lacking front teeth, with a red goatee down to his chest. Lu had come off the streets begging for a place to sleep, same as me. Lu was assigned a bed in my bunk room. He had no income as far as I could see.

Gary: Gary came into the house two weeks after Lu. Gary was 5'7," had black hair, no front teeth, and smelled. Gary bunked with Lu. It was not hard to realize that Gary generated income the same way Lu did. Both were selling and using heroin. Gary knew the street and thrived on it. After overhearing a conversation between Lu and Gary, I realized they sold their bodies for money. I would hear them say, "How much did you get?" "30 dollars!" "Why?" "Hey, I was lucky; I could have used powder to find the pussy!"

Lu and Gary were perfect examples of the subculture of the street and addiction. I learned a lot about the negative influence of the subculture by watching Lu and Gary befriend Andy P. They were constantly talking to and advising Andy while Jim, his father, was out of the building. Andy's personality began to change because of the negative influence. My point is that a person's behavior can be modified by others. These are the people who purposely set out to manipulate, to lead and influence. They are the people to run from.

Hope remains-job search pays off: All the emails and phone calls started to work. A large retail chain and a security company asked me to come in for face-to-face interviews. The convenience store gave me my starting hours. After living through the infection of 2011 and seeing what I saw, I did not doubt the existence of a higher power. Someone or something was still with me!

I took measure of my personal rebuild:

- Housing **Done**

- Part time jobs **Done**

- Long term, high paying job

- Repayment of outstanding debts

- Budget for cash flow and outstanding bills being covered **In Process**

- Move *from* Boston, within the 128 belt, back to the suburbs of the Boro's. **Done**

Securing the jobs and health: I still had the car and all my work clothes in it. This time, I was committed to making my stay at this shelter different. I checked out AA meetings nearby, switched my primary doctor from Boston back to Doctor Ford of the MetroWest, looked for therapy, and went back to karate.

I met with the hiring managers at both companies and was assigned my start dates and hours. It was obvious to most of the tenants and management that I was focused on bettering myself. Since some were trying to do the same, I fit in for the time being.

Fitting in or feeling that you fit in is a good thing. But never let down your guard. What does that mean? Not all the people you live with want others to succeed. They would rather watch you fail, drink, snort, or needle yourself so they can say, "I told you so" or watch you suffer. It is hard to believe that people can act that way and it is even harder to be the target. The two boys at the first shelter were a target, and they lasted two days: they were back on the street of Boston with nothing. Male or female, gay or straight, that is life in the subculture.

Hope leads to Will and Will lead to Planning and Planning leads to Action: JC Penney hired me; I was a natural at selling jewelry. I had never worked in retail, especially at a mall, so I took it as a challenge. The only issue I had was the woman who was to train me. She had her way of selling jewelry for over thirteen years, had her customers, and made sure I knew that she was top dog.

Working security: The security company I worked for subcontracted to a large computer company in Hudson, one town over from

Marlboro. The computer company was downsizing in six months. My job was to cover the desk, drive the car around the property, and secure the facility. It was here I realized something was happening with my body. The shoes I was wearing were hurting me and my right leg was in pain.

It was a street revelation that I was at another dry house that had bunk beds. The transitional housing system gives the tenant time to land a job and get off the state food plans and state insurance system. However, I quickly realized that there is a population in the subculture that embraces the rules and the system. They may never leave, at any age. It was at this point of my street culture experience that I was thrown into and used the system for survival.

Excerpts from my journal:

9-14: I work every day for three companies; washing dishes, driving, and selling jewelry. The manager at the house says I could stay. I get along with most everyone. I do my chores and look forward to my bed. I feel safe now.

9-15: I paid $60 towards the cell phone bill. Johnny called me and thanked me for getting it back. Retail is great. I am fitting in and they like me 90%.

9-18: All is good. Security is moving forward. The bank needs $200 by the end of Sept. to stay away. The convenience store job is dropped; terrible management. I paid the insurance bill from the money from the convenience store job. Plan 3 is working.

9-20: Master Bill invited me back [to the dojo], so I am going to release stress. Dr. Virginia Dwyer has volunteered to be the editor for my book. All blood tests were ordered, and Dr. Ford has brought me back as my primary doctor. He feels I have improved 100%.

9-28: I caught an infection from the bunk room and air conditioner. It is my first sinus infection since the 2011 operation.

9-29: Big News. Dr. Ford said I had an infection. I cannot have any antibiotic with any form of penicillin. That eliminates two-thirds of the antibiotics I have taken for decades. The penicillin will shut down my renal functions and kidneys.

Just think what would happen if penicillin or a derivative of it were given to be me within the last year when I visited LA to see Johnny. The hospital and visiting nurses told me nothing about any after affects.

By the second month at the Palladin Shelter, I was a fixture. I liked the people and *some* of the managers. I treated the managers with the respect they deserved, and understood their "desire to be the man."

Then "the fart:" Our room had settled for the night. We were all in our bunks by the appropriate time, anticipating who was going to snore the loudest. Then without warning a smell permeated the room. Not just your average smell, but one that is known as, a "gag me smell." Tim and his son said, "What the hell." One by one comments were made about the origin of the smell. Then there was a laugh. The laugh moved from one bunk to the next until the whole room came alive with laughter. For ten to fifteen minutes, there were comments, laughs, and more comments. The laughs grew louder and louder. It was as if these men, from all walks of life, bad and good, happy or sad, reverted to the ages of seven to eleven. It was reminiscent of a pajama party or summer camp cabin. For just those minutes, everyone was a child filled with laughter.

When you are at a safe and sober house, there are rules you must live by. If you disobey any of the rules, YOU WILL LOSE THE ROOF OVER YOUR HEAD. Below are five rules. In the first shelter, I broke rules four and five. In the second shelter, I broke rules one and two. Both were initiated or exposed by people who wanted me out of the shelter or worse.

- No disruptive behavior

- No fighting

- No threatening

- No drugs or alcohol

- No coming to the house under the influence

Hope, Will, Planning, and Action Are Gone as fast as they came:

Excerpts from the journals:

10-1: New guys are in the bunk room. Not good. The penicillin discovery is getting to me. I cannot get the security company to change my 11pm hours. The curfew is 10pm. Helene and Ken told me to go sleep in my car.

10-2: Good day but fighting depression. Two six-figure jobs fell through. I am very upset about sleeping in the car.

10-3: I had wine in the car to sleep and reduce my leg pain. Had a negative effect.

10-9: Nightmares again. Guys told me to shut up. Lu getting violent even though I tried to be nice. I called a realtor about rooms. I am holding all the jobs together but plan for jobs are gone. I go to AA as much as I can.

10-10: Physical fight with Lu. I was baited into it. Ruff and Carlos stopped it. It is a throw-out offense.

10-15: Gary, Lu's friend, is still on the top bunk of our room.

Three days after the fight on the tenth, Lu's mat was rolled up and the blankets were gone. As I have mentioned before, it is not wise to ask questions that do not concern you directly. You keep your mouth shut! No one was sorry to see him leave.

On the night of October 19th, I was putting on my security guard uniform in C room. Ruff, Gary, and I were in the room when Gary decided to pick a fight. He wanted to "mix it up" and insisted to fight outside the house. I still had use of my legs; I was sober and happy. All I had to do was use what I knew from my martial arts: arc my left foot while on the ball of my foot, step over that foot with my right leg, turn my back, and then with the left foot throw a power back kick to the chest. But NOT me--I took the high ground. I called management from the next room, told the story, got dressed, and went to work. Six hours later I got back to the house at 12:15 am. I was immediately kicked out by the night manager. I had to leave with what I was wearing, and that night New England was having a Nor'easter rainstorm.

After I called for the manager and left the shelter, Gary had two hours to persuade the managers I was dangerously aggressive. Since these managers had already been disciplined by upper management for ordering me to sleep in my car, it was payback time. I was out in the rain with nothing. A year later, I received supporting material from the police reports and the discharge report from Palladin. Not only did the content not match, neither did the dates. I had been targeted, hit, and knocked out for the count.

Jim was nice enough to drive me to nearest hotel and beg a room to get me out of the nor'easter. While holding my clothes and standing outside the lobby, the police pulled in to question me; I told them what had happened and where I had been living. The police asked, "Are you going to hurt yourself?" "Are you going to hurt someone else?" *My answers were NO and NO.* The police responded, "Well, we cannot do anything!" I said, "Then shoot me." The police said, "That is what we needed." An ambulance was called so I could be taken to the third floor of the Marlborough Hospital for observation.

The police were trying to do me a favor. I knew it, and they knew it. The police knew the shelter very well and believed my story. The police report read, "Upon arrival, I spoke with Brian Masters who stated he was homeless and looking for a free room" at the Embassy Suites. "At this point he was placed under a Section 12 and transported to the hospital."

*All of Massachusetts was buckling down for a three-day, nor'easter rainstorm off the ocean. The homeless have no chance to stay dry, warm, and healthy. But the truth is that the city authorities do not want homeless people dying on **their** streets.*

The Second Institutionalization

I have already described the procedures, rooms, organizational structure, and the profiles of staff and patients of the first hospital where I was institutionalized. The hospital the police took me to be no different than the first, so I will not repeat myself.

The police saved me, but I lost it all: I was admitted to the hospital under Section 12, observation of someone at risk of hurting themselves. A staff guard is placed at the entrance of your room, and you are observed for twenty-four hours. Under Section 12, I could not be released until I had attended classes, been observed, and had meetings with the medical doctors and psychiatrists. There were no cell phones allowed. The patients could only use *one wall phone* which had the *psychiatric caller ID*. I could not report to the security company and, so I lost my job. I just watched the rain fall.

During my stay at the hospital I was required to attend classes. The classes were like what I had experienced at the Davis Group. The Davis Group focused on individuals with substance use diseases. In retrospect, this should have been the first stop in my resolution to understand my issues. Pembrook and most of its third-floor patients had substance use issues combined with solid risk of suicide. These were patients needing serious and focused treatment. Again, these classes taught family and institutional treatment, which has been proven to work. But as I said before, learning is not doing. At no point during my stays, were my fellow patients directed to any such offerings by the state. So much money was invested weekly, month after month, year after year, only to have people be put on the street after only days of treatment.

> Dr. Randal taught one of the more scientific group sessions on substances, the brain, and brain recovery. While Dr. Randal was teaching a class on the duration in which the brain can recover. I brought up the Yale University finding that supported the ninety-day theory and the sleeper effect. Not only was Dr. Randal surprised by my input, he admitted to the classes where the finding came from. Nonetheless, at no point during my stay at the hospital was a long-term plan treatment offered.

I was released from the hospital after four days and drove back to the shelter to get my belongings. Carlos and Ruff had saved my clothes and shoes (except for my $120 Docksiders, which were missing). Ruff physically forced Gary to hand me my custom-made shirt. My meds, locked up by management, were also missing. The transitional housing organization had the monopoly on housing in MetroWest, and I had set all my jobs, living, and plans around living there. Now their housing was not an option.

The Palladin shelter slide: I had been two weeks away from being able to afford my own room. My episode at the Palladin shelter caused the loss of my job at the security company. I started sleeping in my car, washing at McDonald's, and changing in the car. Depression raised its ugly head, and I started using alcohol as a sleeping and pain aid. The retail job was affected by my attitude. You could see it in my eyes, my hands, and probably my smell. When the other employees saw my car in the mall parking garage overnight and me changing in it, I was told, "You are no longer Penney material." Within two weeks, everything I had built was gone.

So, who were the good guys? Ruff, who was a witness to Gary's challenge to fight, said nothing to back me up. I know Ruff did the right thing because he was on probation, and he did not need to be on anyone's radar. His new attempt at life could have been ruined. When you have hit the street and shelters, your future can change in an instant. In my case, the constant changes wore me down. To be institutionalized, lose a job, and be on the street in one day can affect anyone's hope. I was losing hope and the other three, Will-Plan-Action, followed. I would think to myself, "How many of these stories happened?" "How much more can I take?"

By the beginning of November, I was again living on the streets. That meant moving the car from place to place, using the library to communicate and job hunt and sleeping where I could. I had achieved the fruits of my hard work with housing, jobs, bank account, paying bills and not needing money. Now I was nowhere.

Pain: Now the pain in the small of the back and right leg started to stab me hard. First the pain would start at the middle of the thigh in the right leg. Then it would shoot down to my foot; it was a combination of burning pain and itching. All I could do was to bite down on an object and move my body until the pain subsided. My right hip and groin area were in so much pain that the right leg couldn't hold my body weight. Steps were a challenge and climbing a ladder was impossible. Dr. Ford and I thought it was inflammation from my past surgery, so no x-rays or MRIs were ordered.

Adapt or give up: I desperately worked to find housing close to the Boro's and the malls. By November 10th, all my options for housing and potential five-figure jobs fell through. The only shelter available within driving distance of a car or bus was the largest city in Massachusetts with the worst crime in the state. I had to fix my situation on my own. I applied to two retail stores and was hired at Macy's. Training started on the 12th.

On November 13th, Mike brought the perfect clothes that I had requested: an old dirty ski coat to keep me warm, a grubby shirt to pull over my white undershirt, and jeans. He also brought me a small amount of cash. I loved the grubby shirt because it was a green and white Boston Celtics shirt with a rip down the shoulder. The jeans were ripped at the crotch and showed spots of blood stains on the legs.

Journal: "I still will not call for help. I know the family is trying tough love. They do not know the progress I have made without their support. Johnny's comment when I called from the hospital, "just straighten out and get a job," hurt. It reminded me of the Bruce Hornsby song which contains the line, "Get a job."

I Was Writing about Subculture.

Now I Am Part of the Subculture

The First Wet Shelter

An introduction to a wet shelter: From now on, I will mix my story with actual comments taken from the journals I kept. Remember, when you're at this point, your past is gone, and you live for the present.

I cannot share all the pages in the journal about the shelter, but it was where the idea for this book began. Around November 17th, I wrote, "I know that they know, I know too much. Maybe when this is done, I will put the journals into a book."

Later in this book I will outline the life events that I believe temporarily pushed me back to substance use. I will also outline what I feel could be the solutions/keys/actions that could help a person avoid that path. For now, keep walking in the other's shoes.

On November 14th, I drove to the Worcester wet shelter located at 50 White Street, across from the psych hospital. I parked the car in the parking lot and walked through two glass doors and up to the cage where a staff member sat. On either side of me were men wearing old soiled jeans and coats, shaking from the night before.

I walked up without a word and the boy at the front window handed me a form. I told them I was homeless and had no food. Maybe a job is lined up? These are the key elements necessary to convey desperation with hope. I had passed the first test.

The layout of the shelter: A small waiting area on the left was used for sleeping after 9 pm. Three yards up on the left was the electronics and medication holding room; NO electronics or cell phones were allowed in the building. By confiscating the phones, the management knew there would be no fights about them, no stealing them, and no pictures or audio of the reality between six pm and eight am. Those were the hours the men and women were allowed to stay in the shelter.

When you walked five more yards, you entered the cafeteria, which doubled as a cot bedroom after seven pm. On the left was the hallway to the men's bunks and mat room. On the right was a hallway to the offices and the women's bunk rooms.

I was led down the hall to the offices and buzzed in. There were roughly twelve men and women going about their business. Sherry, a case manager, introduced herself, and I sat down. After explaining my past and circumstances, Sherry told me about a program that would provide money up front and move me out of the shelter quicker. I was told that I would get updates from Sherry, to hold tight, and move forward.

It was then that I devised a plan to move the car two streets away. I would sleep at the shelter at night, change in the car, go to work, and drive back at night. Then I would change back into the street clothes, eat if possible, and go to bed.

Journal: "Important. I decided to be just like them. I will not make the same mistake I made at the last two shelters. I will have no pride, not talk unless I have to, look down, and sleep."

I wrote in the journal, "be just like them." Well, I was them! I changed my speech, my walk, and my talk to what the population was used to seeing and hearing. With this change came a "new you:" a survivor in a new world of friends.

The daily morning announcement: Every morning the shelter residents would have to gather in the cafeteria to hear a representative from the transitional housing organization. She would step up on a chair, so everyone could see her, and say the rules only once. She told us:

• to make sure we were out and back in to the shelter at the appropriate times;

• we would have access to our case managers on the assigned days;

• felons, child molesters, abusers, anger management cases, and rapists would be assigned special case managers.

The cafeteria: I scanned the room for a spot that would give me space, so I would not have to engage in a conversation. People wore clothing you might expect to see on homeless street people. Now they were inside. Some of the women wore feathers or carried fake animals for attention and begging food and money. Most people had weeks of old clothes that were not washed and the smell that goes with it. Table manners were the exception. I ate with my hands and looked only at my food.

The first night: The routine was to gather your stuff unless you had a bin; there was one bin per person. You would sit at dinner table at five pm, eat, and wait until six when they closed the doors. Then you would be assigned a bed. People would yell and scream for a spot. I was assigned bunk bed 9-bottom. Once the beds were assigned, the men scrambled for the mats and cots. Every available space was taken in each room and the hallways except the office hallway to the women's rooms.

The showers: The first four days I avoided the showers and cleaned up elsewhere. On the fourth day, I waited until the last minute before the doors closed. Even then, there were men there. You just stayed distant.

Meeting Fred: I was fixing the mat and the sheet on the bunk, so they fit. Then I turned and saw a tall, well-built white man wearing a Boston Red Sox hat move his hand as a signal. I slowly walked over and looked at him. "Man, you do stand out!" he said. "Look, put your coat underneath your mat. Then, when they close the door, wait in the dark, then pull it out as your pillow. If you don't, they will take it now or during the night!" I dropped my head, moved back to the bed, and did exactly as he said.

I get to know Fred: Fred and I would look at each other and not talk. The more people you knew, the more you put yourself at risk. Fred had a fractured foot that was operated on at the hospital, and the operation did not go well. He had worked for his brother and had a Class A trucker's license but no use of his foot, so his brother kicked him out. The shelter was the only place for him to go. Fred had done ten years in jail in the Midwest for running cocaine and weapons for his motorcycle gang. One unlucky night, high on cocaine, he stopped at a bar, got drunk, beat up the bouncer, and fought the cops. Once he was cuffed the bouncers and cops pummeled him. Fred had deep scars on his skull, thus the Red Sox hat.

He said, "Brian, you're doing the right things and do not interfere whatsoever, or you will get it on the street or when the doors close and the lights go out!"

The New England snow was starting to come in, and Fred would have to walk ten blocks to the hospital for meds. There was so much ice one day that I stayed and drove him to the hospital after people had scattered into the streets. We were okay at that point, but *it was my first mistake. I was nice and let my guard down.*

Hope-Macy's retail job: On November 17th, "I went for my last interview at Macy's. Hired!! They were impressed with my professionalism and I was hired; I was offered $8.50 an hour plus commission selling men's suits and shoes. I knew "Chuck Brannock, the inventor of the shoe device you see in shoe stores and friend of my family before I was born," would be happy.

> That night I was on the top bunk in the middle of the room. The staff announced that the medically impaired were allowed some slack and space, then the doors closed. A little man who was suffering from a hernia dragged his mat over near the "fat man." The little man must have been only 5'2" and dying from pain. The fat man, roughly, 280 pounds, loudly told the little man he was too close to his area. The little man did not move. The fat man got up and pounded that man twice with his fists. Then the little man dragged his mat to the middle of the room until someone said it was okay. No one moved to help him. The old me would have jumped from the bunk, laid a kick and punch to the fat man, and that would be it. I laid on my bunk and covered my head with the coat Mike had given me.

Journal: November 18th. I tried to nail down the case workers and make progress out of here. But they think I am a bum, which is what I wanted. I got a bed and made friends with Kelley and Jeff. I must remember to stay in my place. Fred is keeping my secret.

> Another time two women went at it with all fists flying. Someone had stolen something. Once it was broken up, the women were told to get to the women's area. Then the fight started again over the floor mat to sleep on and the spot. In the men's area we were laughing our asses off. One of the men was an older Puerto Rican who had shit his pants and his mat because he was too drunk to get up. Everyone lived with the smell until you fell asleep or the morning arrived, and the staff turned on the lights.

Journal: November 19th. Some are now calling me the quiet one. I changed in the car in the freezing cold. Gas is gold again.

November 20th. It was my birthday and the morning routine was the same. While I was getting air outside, one of the women fighters, twenty-eight, blonde, low-cut blouse, was driven into the lot. The driver was a man in his forties wearing a wrinkled suit. He handed her cash and drove off. I just stared at the sky.

I went to work and came back at the appropriate time. I had no calls from anyone on my cell except Mike. Mike told me I had one card from my brother James at the house and that was it. *My birthday was over. I handed in my cell phone, ate, got a mat, a wet blanket, and talked to no one.*

Reality-hold on tight: The next night I was coming back to the shelter and needed to stop to use a bathroom. I had no clue where I was, but I stopped at a grocery store, still dressed for my retail job.

At least two people hit me up for money and the bathroom break took five minutes.

> When I came back to the parking lot, my car was gone. I watched in horror as a tow truck was pulling out of the parking lot with everything I had in it: laptop, journals, autographs, suits, *everything*. I was able to stop the driver and pleaded to let the car down. "$100 in cash," was his comment. I pulled my phone and said that I would call the police. "Now it is $200 buddy, one for me and one for him. You have five minutes"! I cleaned out my account of last week's wages and gave him cash. He let me have my car.

On Saturday, Fred and I snuck away to get some real food, his treat. While sitting in the car a woman came up and knocked on the window. It was the blonde with the same low-cut blouse I had seen earlier. She asked for five dollars from both or either of us. When we hesitated, she commented that she was in need, *bad*! We gave her three dollars--all we had.

Remember the first page of the book where I asked, "What do you want to do today?" The fighting, begging, blonde is that woman.

My first scar: It was November 26th, I was driving back from work as usual, and I parked two blocks away from the shelter. It was the day before Thanksgiving, and I was out of work early. Tomorrow I was to help the needy back in Westborough, and tonight I would ride out the snowy nor'easter in the shelter. I treated myself to a good CD and rolled down the windows for fresh air. With my eyes closed and music on, a young man came from the driver side and pointed a gun. "We are going to take what we want, so get out." As they reached in, I saw my bag with the journals and the Hollywood autographs Johnny had given to me for the kids' charities. I said," Just don't take that." The pistol came down across my head and I saw a bolt of lightning. Since it was daylight, and I was on my knees, they moved quickly. The only items taken were my new black Dollar Store clothes for the Macy's job, money on the dash, and my cell phone. Nothing else of real value.

I had had enough. I gathered my strength and started the car. The corner had a good liquor store, so I stopped. After feeling less pain, I realized that going to the police was worthless and not a good idea. So, I drove to the shelter, only to realize it was past six pm and doors were locked. I saw the fat man laugh, and I threw him the bird and mouthed, "Fuck you." His mouth dropped; that was my only good memory of the Worcester shelter.

Run for the safety of home: After a quick cleanup and change of clothes, I went to volunteer at a Thanksgiving dinner in Westborough. The cut on my forehead and my unsteady movements made my Civic Club members know that I was the person needing the help. It took time, but I recovered slowly and worked my shift.

Vindication of the Trauma

Ex-wife tells all: At the Thanksgiving dinner, I came in from directing cars and shoveling snow off the walk. Then I saw her, Patricia Landers, the ex-wife of Randy Landers—the guy who beat me. Patricia was there the night of the attack in 2007.

It was as if we had nothing to hide, and the chemistry between us had always been good. I did not hold back and gave her the short version since 2011. Then it was her turn. Patricia confirmed all my suspicions about people and events that I could never get solid proof. I got it all within 45 minutes:

- Linda (my ex) and Randy had been friends after I left the house, and they drank in town often.

- Linda did help Randy's lawyer try to put me in jail with my own medical records.

- Yes, there was a close relationship between them and still is.

- Jennifer, the woman who loved me so much, lost interest as my money depleted and health declined.

- Yes, Jennifer was and still is with the millionaire and will always go for money and security; after 2011, I was a tool.

Patricia had ended the relationship with the contractor in town. She was still friends with Randy and getting by like everyone else. As we spoke of the events and people of the past, we laughed, as if it had been a movie. Then she asked about Mike Garrison. Patricia always liked Mike in a more than friend kind of way but she never followed through. She then told me to call Mike and tell him of the robbery and pistol whipping and ask for help. So, I did. The last words between us were, "Brian, Thanksgiving is not your holiday," and we laughed again. Liz and Mike said, "Come on down." So, I left the Thanksgiving charity meal and drove south to Canton.

Vindication of My Experiences: My history with the Garrisons goes back almost forty-five years. We have shared so many life events that, depending on the person, the attachments could never be destroyed. I stayed with Liz and Mike through the month of December. It was a time to get organized and take the next step. My spirit had taken a beating and life had run me over.

That is why you must turn your path to a positive. Reader, take the "I like and I can do" road. The people, events, and substances may take you by surprise but, for most, you might have a choice.

The month of December blew by like a gentle snowstorm, all good. One-day Mike and I were sitting in his kitchen discussing what had happened and what to do next. Let's face it, no one was going to believe what I had been through, especially at the wet shelter. It was just then I decided to check my old cell phone messages with my new cell phone.

There it was, a voice mail from the people who robbed me. I forgot that when I was sitting in the car recovering from the robbery, a woman came up to the passenger side window. That woman said, "For $40 dollars, you can have your phone back." Now, weeks later, we were stunned and amazed; these people had called me. Now the woman had left a message on my cell, asking for the $40 dollars!

Mike and I just stood in amazement. How could someone be so stupid?

If you are on heroin and you are in need, the body is shaking, and the head is pounding. Anything goes to get that $40 bag.

Right then, all my credibility came back. Now I had verbal proof of my story. I went to the car and got the physical proof of the tow, cash robbery, the ticket for the crosswalk violation, and a selfie of my bloody head. Mike and Liz knew I was telling the truth. It was then I knew a credible book could be written.

Calm Before the Storm

December events:

- I drove to work at the retail store and kept the bills paid.

- I helped with the food and bought the Christmas tree.

- I continued to go to AA and had an occasional drink at the house, especially when the pain in the right leg was at its worst. I would stay downstairs in my room.

- I could not go west, so I found a shelter in Quincy.

- I successfully ended my holiday hours at the store on a good note.

- Mike had gotten my old glasses repaired for twenty dollars. I could see again.

It was at this time that I met with Monsignor John of St. John's church about becoming a deacon. After two meetings he knew I was sincere, but to study to be a deacon costs a minimum of $4,000. Combined with my condition, it was not reality. Then I was introduced to St. Vincent de Paul. After a visit with Mike and me, the two SVdP ministers wrote me a check for $200. With the money, I drove home to central New York, sober, to test a move back.

I realized it was not time to go back to New York. Thousands of dollars of furniture were in storage in Westborough. Health insurance and food were in Massachusetts, and I had something more to do. I became complacent being back in such a relaxed atmosphere in New York. There were so many triggers.

My last mess up: On January 6th, 2015, I drove back from Syracuse, New York with a plan to give back my car to the bank, get an hourly job and an apartment, and let life just happen. No plan three, and no plan four. *I was giving up.* By the time I hit Westborough, I made a stop and drove on. By the time I reached Wrentham, I was legally drunk and driving in the dark. Luckily the woman I rear-ended had just a bump, but the police sent me to the hospital and took the car. Although I was not arrested, my license was suspended on four charges, and I was awarded a new secret RMV charge: *An Immediate Threat.*

Again, my car was towed with everything in it. Mike came to the hospital to pick me up, go to the police station, retrieve everything out of the car, and store everything except one suitcase on wheels. I had picked the Quincy shelter as my next stop. That is where we went on January 13th, 2015.

My Last Wet Shelter – A Hell Hole Meant to Help

Welcome with a smile: On January 13th, I arrived at the wet shelter, probably one of the first of its kind thirty years ago. The procedures were the same, and the intention of the intake managers were the same--help you get a roof over your head so you can help yourself. The intake manager, John, was a straight-forward, heads-up kind of guy. After I told him my plan to get on my feet, John approved my being there. Mike and I said our good byes, *again,* and he drove away. But I was different. I was giving up. I felt it.

When you are on the street, sober or not, and hope fades, so does your will. No matter how strong you were, if you were a fighter, if you had been rich, if you had been abused, "hope" is the lifeline. Without it, each individual fade away in his or her own way. You may think what is about to happen is unreal, but it was real. You fight for life or what is left of it.

John showed me around and introduced me to the staff behind the glass wall. It was a glass wall. The building was small but housed many people. Roughly fifty-six men in the men's bunks and twenty-five men and women on mats in the cafeteria. There was a very small waiting room between the staff glass and the front door, with small benches between the first outside door and the inside door. The inside door was locked until the tenants *had to* leave the building in the morning and come back at night. If you did not come back at night, *you would lose your place at the shelter.*

My second scar: Mike had given me money from my account, so I had something in my pocket. Two blocks away was a McDonalds, so I went and bought a hamburger and extra food for my pocket. The ocean wind had picked up and the temperature dropped to single digits.

I limped back to the shelter and attempted to open the door, but it was locked. I buzzed and knocked on the window until finally one of the staff, irritated by my persistence, came to the outside door. "It is five minutes after hours. After that, the doors are locked" he said. I barely got out the words, "Come on, what do I do?" The staffer walked back inside.

I love and hate the phrase, "You cannot make this up!" I had on light clothing and a coat not made for coastal winds or outside sleeping.

I made my way down the street, looking for some bushes or box to crawl into with my suitcase on wheels. That is when I spotted a pickup truck back in a dark lot. That would get me out of the wind and buy me time to think, so I started walking toward the rear bumper. That is when the young men appeared. It was clear that they wanted my bag and anything else I had; the first man's finger said it all. I hit the first guy, solid in the throat. That gave me time to throw the bag into the bay of the pickup truck, but my timing was too slow. I was hit right in the head and the glasses. I am not sure if the bumper or the glasses cut the gouge in my forehead. That was the last I saw of the young men.

Totally dazed, I climbed into the truck deciding whether to drop or go. I grabbed the bag and hit the ground right when the police cars were stopping on all sides. The blood was coming down on my face and jeans, which prevented me from accurately search for my recently repaired glasses and lens; they were now crushed.

I told the police my story, and they took me to the hospital. The doctors stitched me up and injected fluid for dehydration. One officer asked me again why I was on the street at night. I explained the events of the day as the officer's face showed he was getting pissed, not at me but the circumstances to which I was subjected. An hour later, I was driven by ambulance to the door of the shelter; I was given a blanket and a mat in the cafeteria. The time was 1:14:38 (police time) on January 14th, 2015, as written on the police report.

I woke the next morning at five am listening to yelling by the "staff trustee." He was one of us but he had more privileges. Every morning, if you slept in the cafeteria, you were obligated to:

- Pick up the mat.

- Pile it neatly against the far wall.

- Sweep the floor.

- Mop the floor.

- Roll in the tables.

- Wash the tables down.

- Then shower up with the bunk bed people

If you did not help, you were singled out for the unwritten rule of expulsion from the shelter.

I was a novelty for a week with the bloody bandages over the forehead and blood on the clothes. I decided to act the same way I had in at the previous wet shelter:

- Head in a low position

- Move slowly and never smile

- Always carry your bag, put your head on it, or sit on it.

No one will help if you lose something. No one.

House rules: The word "rules" has two meanings: what you're required to do and the shelter totalitarian rules. The rules were just like at the other shelter about having no devices that could be used to record or photograph. The environment was such that, by turning someone in or being obedient, you got something back - maybe a bunk, a bunk with extras, or an outdoor pass.

Bunk beds: Should you be assigned a bunk, you may or may not have another the next night. Should things go your way and you work with the staff, your bed may go up in the number system. As I wandered between bunk rows, I witnessed men who were tired and weathered. The stench was a combination of dirty socks and the overwhelming smell of chlorine.

Bathroom: When entering the bathroom in the morning, I would straddle the middle of the floor. The shit and piss would be anywhere. The showers were open, just like the other wet shelter, and you are always alert depending on who was near you. Then you dried off. Lack of toilet paper was a problem.

Paul from Pembrook comes back: "My God, how are you?" I yelled out to the familiar Irish face. It was Paul from Pembrook. This was the young man who thanked me and became one of the smiling group after I returned his girl's food money. He had mentioned that he lived in a town nearby and his mother lived there too. He had been a high school football star.

He was very glad to see me, but Paul had all the signs of NOT staying on the path of recovery. His eyes were glazed, his body and hands shook, and there was a hint of desperation; he had made the turn back to meth or heroin. "My mother has had enough", he said. He did not mention the girlfriend.

During the time I was at the shelter with Paul, he hung with some younger men who had the same traits. There was no way I would get close to them, and our conversations gradually ended.

Paul freezes to death? One night there was a Nor'easter, one of many winter storms in 2015. The city of Quincy is on the ocean, guaranteeing high winds and low wind chill temperatures. That evening when I was walking from the cafeteria to the bunk bathroom, I saw Paul at the inner door of the shelter. He was knocking on the door, literally begging to get in for the night. Paul was looking directly at me, crying. Paul then fell to his knees. But I hesitated to move. I turned to the staff behind the glass wall and asked them to open the door or I would. The staffer said, "He was caught with a phone and told to leave. If you open the door, you will be out there too." By the time I turned to the door, Paul was gone.

He had been wearing spring clothes. The snow was falling as he begged. I never saw Paul again.

We think that something like this could not happen. I hoped Paul would be in protective custody like I had been. **Well, we are dead wrong!** *You will hear more of Martin Phillips in the last phase of the book. Martin's cousin had been an alcoholic and lived in the woods of Long Island. One night that cousin froze to death during a snowstorm and high winds from the Atlantic Ocean. Reality is what I am attempting to provide you. It happens.*

My Turn to Die?

We suffer from a place as well as weather:

Journal: The environment is like hell shelter. Guards should never go to church. This is becoming my life. You ride with it or you die.

That winter weather was one of the worst in years. This meant that the shelter had to allow one of the rules management and staff did not like. The rule was, "<u>weather inclement housing.</u>" In other words, if the temperature was so low and the snow, fog, and ice were unsafe, the shelter had to allow men and women to stay inside between 8 am and 6 pm.

We were dirty, tired, beaten, and just waiting for something. Staying there gave me the opportunity to observe different people. There were men and women of all ages. They cradled their heads in theirs arms, used clothes as pillows, and wore backpacks. Some were playing cards and others just talking.

The staff trustee's job was to enforce the rule that people did not sleep during the day. The shelter being open due to the weather was not an opportunity to sleep before lights out. They would yell or touch you, so you would keep to the rule.

Some of us were connecting by talking, others would work up a smile when their eyes caught each other. No TV, no food, and no communication devices were allowed.

I left as I came-in an ambulance: I had proven myself in the eyes of the staff trustees and those behind the glass. I had made it to the back bunkroom, which only had only six bunk beds and a mattress. Men could pass a bottle without getting abused or caught.

One morning, I woke up feeling funny. I could barely get out of bed and everything was a struggle. While sitting in the cafeteria, I realized that I was going to pass out, but I knew I could not. If a hospital staff or doctor were to give me penicillin or a derivative of it, I would lose my renal system, kidneys, or more. So, just like Paul, I knocked on the glass and told the staff that I was sick. It fell on deaf ears. I literally held myself against a wall. One lady, on a bench, leaned against me to keep me up. Again, the staff did nothing. My Higher Power, God or your choice, was watching over me; John, my intake manager, had come into work that day. When he walked by me, I grabbed his sleeve and I told him my problem. I begged!

An ambulance was called, and I was taken to the hospital. The diagnosis? Dehydration, malnutrition, complicated by full-blown pneumonia. I had time before passing out to tell the EMT's and Doctors about the 2011 operation and what happens if penicillin enters the body. *I saved my own life.*

I left that hell hole behind.

The Garrisons' fix to the Quincy shelter's sickness: My next stay with the Garrisons was short. Just long enough to reestablish the funds needed to make my next move. Mike made it very clear: "You cannot go back to a shelter!" Though he may have said it, I knew it.

By the time I was off antibiotics, I had decided where to go. There was the only one logical place. I knew the streets, the medical resources, the mall, and most importantly, the bus transportation for thirty miles.

As the pneumonia cleared up, it became clear that my mind and body were reaching their limits. I googled all the hotels and rooming houses in my target city and there was only one that was affordable; The Burger Hotel.

At this point, the short stay at Mike's was a brief refueling of my mind and body from normal living. If there is a ladder of life and hope is the first rung, I was well below it. In my mind, I had no business friends, no family, no wife, no partner, and I was not sure of my son. Within seven months, I had:

- Been on the street four times

- Been in an institution or hospital four times

- Been in a dry house one time

- Been in a dry and wet shelter four times

- Known three friends that were dead or missing

- Experience three relapses

Yet, somehow, I powered myself for a next move.

Private Public Housing

The Burger Hotel

My first day: It was mid-February 2015 and the administrative assistant of the Burger Hotel had my application and background check approved by the owner, Dick. Dick owned about five houses between Marlboro and the Cape, all rented to low-income individuals and families.

The rent per week was eighty-five dollars. I had money in the bank to pay the rent courtesy of Martin and Mike. I would have my own room as a home base, a place to keep my journals, read, sleep in my own bed, and get a TV and cable. As I looked at it, The Burger Hotel should provide hope.

Hope: I could have:

- A roof over my head – my own room

- Money in the bank

- A part time job to cover expenses

- Time to search for a good paying sales job

- Choice of organizations for therapy and work

- Support structure of people

Mike and I walked up the stairs to the first floor of the hotel. We turned left and saw a long hallway with numerous doors. We walked down the hallway and there was only one door opened, so we knocked. "Is this the manager's office?" The answer was, "Yup." The walls were covered with bedspreads like you would see in a college dorm, as well as an assortment of swords and bayonets.

Mooch, the manager, was in his sixties, a solid, 5'5" man and a former Marine, with tattoos over most of his body.

I sat in front of Mooch's desk, and Mike stood over my right shoulder. He read Mike and me the rules:

- No drugs or the police will come

- No dealing

- No fighting

- Lost key is $45

- All rent is paid in cash, no exceptions

As Mooch went to get his receipt book, I looked down at the floor and started crying again. Mike put his left hand on my right shoulder and said, "It is only a short time. Just till you get back on your feet." I knew, *now*, where I was, and I could show no weakness; I cleared the tears. We gave Mooch the first and last payment in advance, got the hand-written receipts, got the key, and left.

Mike and I went down to the car and pulled out the suit bag, two small cases, a brief case and some food. The hotel must have been built in 1886 or 1887, based on the width of the hallway walking up the stairs and a lack of amenities such as an elevator. Mike and I got to the second floor, walked across the hall and down the hall to get to the next door. We passed some of the rooms with the doors open, but you could not see anything inside. The trip to the third floor was the same except when you came through the third-floor door, the smell of the community bathroom hit your nose and people were standing outside room number 30. Mike and I were literally being looked at like cattle on the way to slaughter. The men had the same appearance as my mates from the previous places I had lived.

The room was ten feet by fourteen feet. There was one window, a small tabletop refrigerator, a single bed, one chair, and a small closet. The microwave was missing. I walked Mike down to the car, we said our goodbyes, and he drove off. I walked up the stairs to my room. You could not walk down the hall without passing room 30. Within a second, a voice came out of room 30. "Welcome to the hotel. I am John King. Do you need anything to get settled"? After a brief exchange of introductions, I mentioned I was planning on getting cable for the computer. "Then you need a TV?" "I can sell you one for ten dollars." As I was explaining that I had no money, one of the young men in the room had gone to the back. He came back with a TV in his arms, walked down the hall and placed the TV outside my door. John King said, "Do not worry about the money, pay me a little bit at a time." I put the TV inside my room, closed the door, looked at the ceiling, and stared. Within ten minutes of being alone, in the hotel, I had been taken for ten dollars for a TV that may not even work.

I spent five and a half months at The Burger Hotel. I had truly been in the Street Culture. The whole concept of Street Culture had not sunk into my brain until living in my car and woods. My spirit had started to break due to the incredible events being thrown at me; yet, I kept going.

You can see the changes in my desperation and outlook by comparing the goals in my journal from July 2014 and the downsized goals of February 2015--just a period of eight months.

Changing Goals

July 2014	February 2015
Self-diagnosis: • Alcohol abuse to mask depression	• Roof over my head – my own room • Money in the bank • Small part time job to

• Depression • Acute loneliness	cover expenses • Time to search for any job • Choice of organizations for therapy and work • Support structure of people
Therapy: • 2 weeks understanding of personal issues • AA arrangements • Physical and mental plan • Friend and family support	
Personal Rebuild: • Housing • Part time jobs • Long term, high paying job • Repayment of outstanding debts • Budget for cash flow	

and pay bills • Move from the Boston area within the 128 belt, back to the suburbs of the Boro's.	

It can be concluded that the environment, uncontrolled events, my self-imposed actions and the failure of the health system reduced me to basic survival. The desire for diagnosis, therapy, and most of my personal goals was gone. Although I had been in four specialized institutions that had focused group and health care initiatives, I was never given the time and the resources to reach my objectives.

The detail from my journal entries during my stay at The Burger are too long to include here. Instead I will explain the highlights in chronological order. The people living at the Burger Hotel had struggles and there were those who would be there for life. Should you not like what I describe, straighten up and fly high. Be happy for what you have.

The first night: I put my clothes away and organized what I had and what I needed. The most important list was the appointments. I knew that I had to have the final interview with Sears, visit the church rectory, find AA, look for the food pantry, find free community dinners, and arrange therapy.

It was time for bed, so I started reading one of the books I took from Mike's house. It was a spy novel, the second James Bond, but not an Ian Fleming book. Around eleven, I set the alarm and put the lights out.

> One hour later, the yelling of a drunken Irishman filled the narrow hallway. I mean, this man had the Irish accent, and he was pissed. He and another man were arguing about being boxers growing up on the eastside of Boston.

The argument had to do with fighting in the ring. The man in room 42 argued that he wanted out and would not go back. "We box, make more money, get hurt, go as an enforcer to make money, and die." The argument lasted roughly an hour and a half until the room 42 man laid the drunken Irishman out in the bathroom. One person asked, "Are you going to leave him there with his feet outside the shower?" An hour later, the pissed-off drunk got up again and pounded on the doors. This time he was punched out near the third-floor door, and I could hear him rolling down the stairs. "He won't come back now," one person said. "He always does," said the other.

I wish I had made a recording or taken some pictures, but if I had, I would have been thrown down the stairs with him. The next day, a very well-built white man with slicked-back black hair came out of room 42. We acknowledged each other and said hello. I believe he was the man who wanted out of life as a boxer in Boston. He had a good man's smile and he left days later.

The first week: The nights went on like that all week: music, yelling, doors slamming, and deals being done. But I ignored as much as I could and slept as many hours as I could. Unfortunately, my diet was poor and I was losing weight.

My first interview at the department store went extremely well, and I was hired to work in jewelry with Eleanor as my manager. Eleanor was in her late fifties or early sixties and had managed that department for roughly twelve years. When we met, I knew she would make the jewelry manager at Penney's look like a happy nun. I road back and forth from the mall on the bus. I was careful not to let anyone see me getting on or off the bus in front of the store. Jewelry sales, according to Eleanor, was all about impression.

On my walks into the city, I found the ARK house on Main Street, where the AA meetings were held, and went to the organizations that ran the MassHealth therapy. Each day was the same and I started to forget who I had been and what I had owned. Even here I could not be myself or risk being singled out. I walked almost everywhere. The weight of the back pack started to take its toll on my feet, legs, and back.

One afternoon I was sitting on my bed looking at the room, my stuff on the floor, nothing in the small frig, and music in the hallway. I studied the walls, ceiling, and closet for gaps or edges, something I could get a rope or my belt around and hold my weight. There was only one hook was high enough off the ground that might do the job. I made my belt into two loops, one for my neck and the other for the hook. I climbed up one foot off the ground and positioned the loop on the hook and the other around my throat. It felt weird, very surreal. *Then there were two knocks at the door.* I was stunned and frightened; getting caught would land me in a hospital you do not come out of. It was Mooch at the door. He came up two stories to see if I was okay. My brother James, Mike, and Martin had not heard from me, so they called the hotel to check on me. I told Mooch that everything was fine and I would call everyone. I unlopped the belt and sat on the bed. Something somewhere had reached out again, so that was the end of that.

I had another problem in the Street Culture! A good number of the men thought I was an undercover cop. During the first week, outside King's apartment, I introduced myself to the group of guys that normally huddled around the door. "You're a cop aren't ya?" "I can smell and feel out a cop!" This came out of a guy who looked like

Gary at the other shelter. "No, I am not a cop, am I, John?" John King hesitated, smiled, and said, "Cool it, he is not a cop." I knew right then that John was on parole. He was not sure I was or was not police, and John wanted no problems. I later nicknamed John "King Rat" after the next book I read.

Inside the building: I decided to be outside the *state housing system*. I was now in the commercial housing system whose rules were those of any socially accepted housing for profit. This environment, floor by floor, had a lifestyle of its own. Depending on the person or people renting the room, that lifestyle might be low-key prostitution, alcohol, drugs, a place to hide, or a place to exist.

For me, the best time to take a shower and do what most would call normal things was between seven and ten thirty am. After that, those who had been in the halls the night before partying, or the individuals who had to get out of bed after the meth or heroin had run its course, came out to commiserate and plan how to get money for the next night.

The tenants who came out in the *early* morning were men and women who were contractors, worked retail, wanted jobs, or had probation requirements. Some rooms you never, ever, saw the person living there. In other rooms, especially on the second floor, most were men who left their doors open a majority of the time and played music. The police were called or came like clockwork every week, if not every third day. The owner of the building provided the police and court system with keys and the legal right to enter at will.

> One morning I gathered my wash kit and opened the door to see five police men and women with a floor resident against the wall. By now, I was not even fazed at what I saw, but I was not sure how to cut through to the bathroom. One of the policeman took his right hand, gestured with his hand and put it to his

chest. I was free to cut through and be on my way.

Outside the building: It was an eye opener and shock to realize how different my life had become in seventeen months. I had lived in three cities and the outside existence was similar in each:

• A vast majority of the men and woman had grown up in those cities and still had friends, family, and children in the neighborhood.

• Your style of dress and the pace of your walk identify you. My walk was a limp with signs of pain, torn pants with blood stains, and a backpack.

• Individuals gathered at the library, the social centers and parks. That is where valuable information is exchanged.

• As women and men would climb the ladder of substance use you could visually see the terrible effects on their bodies and their movements.

• Men and women will find refuge in the woods around the city. This is an asset because it provides shelter and physical safety. They will protect it.

> While walking back along Route 85 from a meeting, I stopped at McDonald's restaurant for some water and the restroom. There at one of the tables was Benny with my backpack. Benny had stolen it from me when I blacked out on a park bench. Now sober and trying again, Benny *knew* I wanted it and the contents, NOW, Benny was stunned, shaking from not having alcohol and eye glazed and red. He took me deep into the woods to a wooden lean-to he called home. There I saw my journals, pens, and brushes. The food and

119

drinks were gone. Benny said he read the journal and was extremely impressed; "That Mike guy is a pretty good guy," he said. I felt stupid for losing what I had protected with my blood and then have someone violate my privacy. I gathered my stuff and we shook hands. I tried never to make enemies on the street.

Reaching out to the church: I was dressed in torn street clothes, my eyes were glassy, my skin pale, and my hygiene bad. It was at the church where I had found help in the past, so I gave it a chance again. I met with the pastor and told him my history and my desire for the future. I asked if I could be involved in the church in some way: labor or ministry which would make me part of something. Father's response was, "Why don't you get on your feet first." Father went out of the room and returned with an envelope. We said goodbye. I promised that I would be at mass on Sunday and walked back to the street. When I looked in the envelope, there was a $10 gift certificate to the greasy spoon on Main Street and $40 in cash. I stopped, I looked back, I swore, and I went directly to Shelley's Liquor Store for a better bottle of vodka.

I cannot stress enough the seriousness of the Street Culture lifestyle. If not for a few jobs and good friends coming to the table financially, I was, potentially, a dead man walking. I would succumb to "anything for a buck or fade away." If you took a sample population of street people, you would find all walks of life, from electrical engineers to contractors to sales people to executives. I failed to put the survival and revival pieces together. I had lost hope.

Hold tight with me as we look at the experience of the young and old, and the difference "one day at a time" can make. I will take direct quotes from my journals to underscore the comments I made on the first page of this book and the reality you can walk straight into, eyes all a glaze.

Working a Plan Again

Selling jewelry: Having a room of my own was perfect for dressing in a suit and leaving for my job at Sears. The snow heaps were high by the beginning of March, the temperature was in the single digits and the wind was brutal. I had to walk around the mall to the employee door in shoes; I had no boots. I entered the store and made my way to the jewelry department. It was then I realized where I was. I was comparing the two stores in which I had worked to a totally different atmosphere. Professionalism was left at the door.

It was my training period and Eleanor held my job in her hand. It could have been the fact that her register count was not the same as mine at close out: "You can't count!" Was it being yelled at in front of other employees for walking out the front door and not using the employee door? Or was it the fact that when I cut my finger on a case, she said, "Leave and do not bleed on my rug." The second week I went to the store manager for my hours; he informed me I had none. The store manager closed the conversation with, *"But please come back and shop at Sears."* I lasted for $486.83 worth of hours.

Stand and brush it off: I was depressed to say the least, and I could not get the past out of my head. Yet, I was holding my own with sobriety- leaving early, going to the Serenity Center, Church, therapy, library, reading, and occasionally enjoying a visit from Mike or Martin. One March weekend I decided to do my wash. That meant going to the second floor which, compared to the third floor, was party central. While putting the load into the dryer, the guys and gals in the hallway asked me if I would like a drink. I felt that this might be the time to adjust to the environment by knowing the people. After the drink, I realized that I was one quarter short and went to the third floor to get my money. That was the last thing I remember until the police were putting handcuffs on me and reading me my rights.

Street survival comes in many forms. People can be violent like the young adults I mentioned earlier or those who have smiling faces and watch you crash and burn while they laugh. Remember, some young man thought that I was an undercover cop; that guy and his friends had been living on the second floor. There would be nothing funnier or more gratifying than to see a cop go on a trip in the building he was watching. I put up a half-assed fight in the jail, and I was seeing things that scared me to death. The officers saw my behavior and sent me to the 3rd floor of the Marlborough Hospital; AGAIN. Thank my Higher Power that an officer of the court was in the emergency room at the time; he spotted me, heard my comments about being drugged and asked me where I lived. When the police heard the name "King" they all turned and faced a wall. They knew! All the charges were dropped.

The last institutionalization: So that I would not hurt myself, I was again sent to the third floor of the Marlborough Hospital and watched for twenty-four hours. It was exactly like I had described when I was framed at the other shelter except for the people I met. My roommate was a young man named Evin. Having been addicted to heroin, he had been doing his best to get medical attention and shake his addiction. The day we were to be released, Evin was clear-eyed and he had a fantastic, go forward, clean attitude. Evin, out of all the people I have known or met in my life, *I believe I inadvertently hurt*. While Evin and I were being discharged, he asked where I lived and how much it cost, so I told him--The Burger Hotel.

When I returned to the Burger Hotel, I met with Mooch to pay my bill. He knew all about my being pulled off to jail and the events leading up to it. I asked him point blank, "Was I given a Micky"? Mooch nodded his head and told me to take care of myself: in other words, "What the hell are you doing here? Watch it!" When I went back to room 43, I saw that the clothes I had loaded into the dryer were folded neatly on my bed. It was the second-floor men and women saying they were sorry after seeing and confirming that I had been arrested. They had been wrong about me being a cop. I never had a problem in the building again.

The next day, as I was coming out of my room, I almost ran directly into Evin from the hospital. He was all smiles and thanked me for telling him about the hotel. Between the money he and his girlfriend had in the bank and food stamps, they were good for a few months. The girlfriend had left rehabilitation on the Cape so she could be with Evin when he came out clean; she was still using. The Burger was the perfect hotel for failure.

Walking the streets: During the last part of March and most of April, I was living on the streets. My son Johnny was paying the cell phone bill completely now, and Mike was watching the bank account like a hawk. So, I got rides to Labor Ready to get money for paying the rent and hitting Sherry's Liquors. I would leave the Burger when the Serenity Center opened and eat my snacks and lunch there. Dinners were provided at two of the churches off Main Street. The goal every day was to stay out of the hotel. I knew that I would either move to a killer drug or just die there. I was a fixture on the street now. I was acknowledged by most everyone from the volunteers to those whose livers were about to shut down. I kept walking.

I had been at the Serenity Center for most of the day, doing my utmost to stay out of the hotel. I had made enough money and my allowance from the bank to make a stop at Sherry's. It was a large bottle I had grown into. Walking back to the hotel, the pain in right leg became too much, and I sat on the bench in front of the church. While sitting, I heard a scratching sound to my left and behind the bushes. As I pushed the branches aside, there was George, whom I knew from the street and the center. George looked me right in my eyes with fear. George was either uncovering or hiding his vodka bottles. He was scared that I knew of his hiding spot and that I would take his vodka. I went back to my backpack and looked at what I had. I could give him vodka or cinnamon rolls. I approached him as you would a scared child and I told him, "This is for you to eat, I see nothing and know nothing." George nodded his head and smiled. I continued walking to the third floor of the Burger Hotel.

As we walk through the people and events, a common fact keeps popping up. There is no personal support for individuals, including me. Yes, there has been and will be family and friends, but those people seem to be on the sidelines looking in. There is no interaction every day or every week. The comments I listened to either at a center, AA meetings, group therapy at the hospital or the street were similar: people's families and friends all were on the angry side.

The other important element mentioned early in the book is that Hope comes hand in hand with support. For example, my request to help the church went unheard. Not from intent but from stigma or ignorance. That hope of giving which motivated me was shot to hell. Take Evin--his support was helping his girlfriend who was far from wanting to shield herself from heroin. All this time Hope and Will dwindled away.

Stigma and Pain are Too Much to Take

One last attempt at Hope and Will: While working at the Serenity Center, I befriended a man named Jerome. Jerome was black, had a good build, was a great cook, good conversationalist, and quick on his feet. Though he had struggled with crack, he had come back to help his daughter grow. Jerome saw that I had been struggling for a source of income and he suggested I apply at a chain store that sold brand names at reduced prices. I used the computer at the Serenity Center, sent my resume, and got a response for an interview.

Journal - beginning of May 2015:

• Ann the scheduling manager seems to be giving me twenty to twenty-five hours. This is enough to keep paying the rent and keep fighting.

• My routine does not allow drinking, so my energy is good and my mind is clear. I have a way to go.

• My schedule is: wake up, pray, go to either the Center or the library, work, AA, and the Center. Hotel to snack and read. Simple but it works.

I was working at a neighborhood store, which meant most employees and customers knew the city. We had managers who understood the importance of working and the repercussions if things went wrong. I had such a manager named Nickoly. For example, when Nickoly was at a stop light and I walked by with a painful limp and backpack, he sounded the horn and waved. Not once did he respond with the stigma, "he is one of them." Everything went well on the job front. The managers, Ana and Tim, ran things by the book because they were scared to death of regional management. Hell, I could have run the store.

Journal: May 15t:h and 16th: Hours run from four to six hours with a ten or twenty-five-minute break. No sitting. You must be ready for the next customer with a smile. The pain in the legs and back is getting acute, so I stretch and move. I have made friends with Adrian, Brandon, and most of the others.

Journal: May 19th: Pain is worse.

Journal: May 21st: Mike, Martin, and I are going to court for the first time. I have a public defender, Sandra, who, I was told, is the best. I must face the driving while impaired. Martin brought me back to town. It is great to be around normal people.

Journal: May 25th: Normal work day, but I was pulled to the office. I was told that I was too slow and needed to improve bagging. I suggested bagging bread as we were taught at the where Price Chopper I had worked before. Not to put bread on the bottom or it will get crushed.

Journal: May 27th: Something is up. Tim, the manager of the store, wanted to talk to me. So, I attempted to talk. He stated, "I will get to you on my time." I know something is up.

I was asked upstairs. I sat at the end of the conference table. Ana, Tim, Rick, and Nickoly sat at the other end. I was spoken to condescendingly:

- I am too slow

- I do not bag correctly

- On May 19th, my register was $10.50 short

- I was insubordinate to Ana about bagging the wrong way

- Due to point system, I should be terminated

- But, Tim will give me a 15-hour <u>retraining</u> opportunity. If he felt that there was no improvement. I <u>would</u> be terminated at his discretion.

- I must sign all the documents now!

- I agreed. I had no choice. Total humiliation. I put the pen down and said, "No one has ever questioned my integrity." I teared up.

I went down stairs with Nickoly and picked my trainer, Adrian, and then finished my shift.

In my defense, I had checked the executive management of the store and the vision statement stated that the employee and *customers should be treated the way you would want to be treated. The men at headquarters were my age or younger, especially the CEO. I was torn between laughing at what just happened because it was so bad professionally, or just doing nothing. I did neither. I recalled that just five years ago I was reporting to the VP of Sales and reporting over $100,000 income on my tax return. Now I could hardly walk back to the hotel, having to bear acute pain.*

I knew that it was a no-win scenario and was mentally crushed. As I walked slowly back to Main Street, I had to make the decision to play the game or do something. What would I have done years before? So, I decided to call the CEO and explain the situation. While walking, I stopped at Sherry's with my first paycheck and bought a bottle.

The next day I received a call from an executive in Human Resources named Tim. I was awarded twenty hours of pay and we agreed to part company. His last comments were, "If you need to reapply or a reference, call me."

For a split second I felt like my old self again.

A month later, I was working at the Serenity Center and Jerome walked up to me. "I do not know what you did but there is hell going on at the top." My call and conversation created a shake-up. It was a touch of gratification in a world of hurt.

June in a nut shell: I did not truly recover from the humiliation. I would walk the streets and go to the Center. I did accomplish interviewing and was offered a job at CVS, but I needed a car.

Journal: June 18th: I called Johnny but got no response.

Journal: June 19th: Mike and his brother Tom worked on their father's house on Martha's Vineyard. I missed that.

Journal: June 20th: No card at Mike's for Father's Day. Will Johnny call?

Journal: June 21st and after: Every night are cops and ambulances. Food. I eat baloney and candy.

Journal: June 25th: Police here every day, and Rick is dead. He fell down the stairs and brokaye his neck.

Physically I was a wreck. My left side was burning, and the right leg had intense shooting pains; I can only explain it as itching with pain, from the knee to the foot. One evening, I bought a bottle of vodka and poured one third of it into a pan; then I put my right foot in it to stop the itching and pain, but it did not work. I had lost ten more pounds with an excellent probability that I had malnutrition.

The third scar: While returning from the Center, I would often stop at the city commons and sit on the bench remembering better times. Benny, who needed something to reduce the body's need for meth or heroin, asked me for the help from vodka. Now that I had come to understand the requirements, I helped him get through the vomiting and minimal seizures. Simultaneously, I was masking the spine and hip pain that had joined the agony of the right leg.

I offered to provide Benny food, so we walked five blocks to the hotel. While crossing the street, I blacked out. For the second time since coming back to town, I woke in the hospital emergency room. The story goes that my right leg collapsed and my forehead hit the street's curb with all the weight of my body. The doctor told me that I was lucky, the stitched split in the skin was covered by an eye brow; the nerves would hurt like hell, but the scar should not show.

Benny later told me that people on the street were laying claim to my backpack, and all he could do was to connect with the individual who stole it. On the last week of June, it cost me sixty dollars to get back my backpack which contained x-rays, reading glasses, hairbrush, vodka, and a journal. When it was returned, it contained the x-rays and a journal.

To this day, I feel that I had been pushed.

The trauma of misinformation: By July 16th I could only walk five blocks to the Serenity Center and one more for liquor. The vodka would kill the pain and keep my head alert for a short time. Then I could move to the church dinners and hang at the Center. It was at the Serenity Center that one of the managers pulled me aside and told me that I was borderline having "Wet Brain." If I did have it, there was no reversing the syndrome, and I would just keep drinking. *There were three things he saw happening to me: jail, hospital, or death.*

In my physical and mental weakened state, I believed this person who specialized in recovery. I was told there was no recovery from my drinking, and I was to drink forever. I believed it. I went back to the hotel and sat on my bed for hours. It was only till the screaming and yelling in the halls came to an end that I had time to think for myself. I kept remembering that I had a lost friend and a neighbor because they did not wait one more day.

• My next-door neighbor in central New York shot himself from depression, no job, and no hope. The next day, he received a job offer. He left his daughter, my ninth-grade classmate, behind.

• My good friend was the brother of a very close high school friend. We were to work together for the summer, and he called me about the job. I told him that I had not heard yet, and I cut the call short because my mom needed some help with the car. The next day I was told that we had the job, and I called his room with the good news. He had shot himself dead. I never saw it coming.

Journal: My decision was taking the last sleeping pill from the hospital and one more day. I went to bed.

Misinformation sparks "the knowledge path": On July 17th everyone at the Center saw my shakes. I brought up the conversation about Wet Brain again and received the same response. I may have been in the worse condition, but I was not happy with the diagnosis. I went to the library and researched:

- Alcohol effect and Wet Brain Syndrome

- Shakes

- Action that can be taken to stop both

I will not go into the three pages of findings from my journal, but actions can be taken on the Wet Brain (Wernicke-Korsakoff Syndrome). It is reversible through sobriety, vitamins, and diet.

Journal: July 18th: The shakes were bad but I got more work done. Mike called to check up on me. I also spoke with Martin on my progress. But one day brought me back. I had been getting violently sick to my stomach and nothing to eat.

The people in this environment were looking for an easy answer to years of substance use to the body and to the mind. Whether it was in therapy, AA meetings, or other courses, many people were not just fighting genetic impulses but years of abuse at the hands of others. Alcohol and drugs were merely masking the pain. At this point, there were none of the survival options around me or my street friends except the Serenity Center; the center is a modern, walk-in, peer to peer meeting place. But now, only a miracle could save me.

The pain is too much: The pages of the journals were repeating themselves, and writing was a thing of the past. The parties in the hallway were happening almost every night and were loud as they could be. The toilets had shit splatter on the seats and vomit on the floors.

The pain on the right side of the body and the right knee to foot would not allow me to walk down the fifty-three stairs and then back up the fifty-three stairs with a loaded back pack. There were only a few familiar faces on the floor that I knew anymore: King Rat, Evin, and occasionally Benny. I had not seen Evin's girlfriend in a while. The last time I heard her voice was on a Sunday morning screaming at Evin to "get something." Evin ran up and down the hall begging money from anyone. An hour later he returned to the floor and all was quiet from his girlfriend.

> Now I was crippled, and I could not make it to the street. So, I opened the door to the hallway when the early party was going. I gave Evin a $20 bill and asked him to get a bottle of vodka, food, and told him to use some money for himself. Two hours later, I was in tears and went out into the hallway to see if he had returned. He had never come back and the comments from the partygoers were, "Forget it man."

It was during one of those nights that I called Martin late in the evening. I had been drinking but the pain would not go away. In a drunk, I was crying again, explaining to him that the pain was unbearable. After we hung up, I passed out and that cured the problem. I slept on my back, and the spine seemed good for another morning.

By now you might be saying, "Why doesn't his brother or friends call the police or an ambulance?" It is the best that they did not. This would have put the police in a bind. Either let it be, take me into protective custody, or arrest me. No matter how good a person you are, you never call the police or get them involved unless necessary. The results could be eviction from the only place that would take a person like you or result in you being labeled psychologically unsound and thrown into a place like the psychiatric hospital's third floor. I needed something else entirely.

I am extracted from the Burger Hotel: My court date of July 28th was closing in, and my system had to be alcohol free, eyes bright, and speech clear. Considering the importance of the court and my cries over the phone, Mike and Martin came to the Burger Hotel. We gathered my briefcases and clothes that I needed and left the hotel.

131

Court: Martin, Mike, and my attorney went to the District Court to face what needed to be done, under the law, for my first driving mistake in forty-three years. Considering my income statement, prospects for a job, and my medical condition, the court dropped all costs associated with classes necessary to demonstrate to the state that I was fit to drive again.

Mike and Martin realize my pain: It was not my choice, but I had no choice. Mike and Martin were calling the shots. I lined up an orthopedic surgeon. It was then that I could go to a hospital without fear of being sent to the psychiatric floor. I welcomed the x-rays and MRIs. I knew, I just knew, that walking through snow and ice heaves, carrying a heavy back pack, and climbing stairs would destroy my body's frame.

All this time Mike and Martin had their doubts about me. One evening I was in such pain at Mike's house that I crawled into a fetal position and cried the pain away. Mike opened the door and saw me. In that instant, I could see the amazement and the glance around the room for booze: "Is he faking?"

I was again taken to the hospital. The doctors reviewed the charts, MRIs, and notes. The doctor sat down with Martin and told him, "He has a wrecked back and his hip is obliterated with no tissue remaining." Of course, only then did the doctors come to me. I was admitted for an emergency operation on August 28th.

The left leg had been taking the punishment for the inabilities of the right leg. As I masked the pain with alcohol, the right leg was taking the punishment for the inabilities of the left leg. Due to my determination to get back to my old world, I held the hourly jobs in retail. That meant standing hours on end. Compounding the condition, I walked miles every day with a backpack weighing ten to twenty pounds, across snow heaves, without rest. Walking up and down the Burger Hotel's fifty-three stairs over a five-month period was a small miracle. For all those years, the mistakes of the 2011 operations were waiting to come back with a vengeance.

I required a hip replacement. For months, the joints had been bone on bone. I, of course, said yes to the operation. The hip surgeon and the OR staff reviewing their part in the operation said the same thing. "Hip operations are done every day and within a week to a month, you will be back to normal." The top spine surgeon's and staff said the same exact thing in 2011!

Interlude

I always liked the myth of the Rise of the Phoenix, especially the movies and books depicting a disastrous circumstance and death. During the situation a far-out idea and a spark of hope emerge, which generate will and a plan of action. This leads to success and a brand-new start.

I believe the beginning of the institutionalization caused by my physical deterioration could have been completely avoided. Had the substance use professionals followed the mental and physical 90-day recovery period recommended by Yale University, my path would have been much different. Yet, I might have missed the people and events I have experienced and, therefore, missed the insights I have gained. I hope these insights will help change lives for the better.

Phase 3 --
A Hospital; A Rehab; A Transitional House; A Home

Highways toward Redemption

We have witnessed a few of the single roads to addiction; it may take only one road and/or contributor for many people. For you and me there is a highway of paths to recovery. I experienced those paths either accidently or by planning action "to do" goals. Redemption was and still is a requirement of mine, so I want to you to discover the paths with me as I experienced them. When I look back at the events between 2007 and mid-2015, the term for survival moving forward is "Redemption." Two definitions of Redemption came up through Google; the definition that pertains to my circumstance is, "the act of making something better or more acceptable"!

When we consider divorce, losing loved ones, any form of trauma, losing a job, financial ruin, or contracting a deadly infection, any one of these events could thrust a person to abuse substances as a way of masking the mental and/or physical pain. That is why this book pertains to anyone, if not everyone. It just happened that I faced the reality of many life-changing events.

In Phase 3, I describe my move into another form of housing. Within each move, I was presented with opportunities to create a foundation of tools necessary to recover. Either I saw the chance and I took it, or held a pure belief that good things do happen. I would like you to discover these opportunities and the importance they bring to survival. My learning experiences from the 2011 operation and all the events in Phase 1 and 2 come full circle in Phase 3. Almost all the people and places will be revisited providing *a view of choices that can be made for good or bad. The benefits for you and me will be real solutions to the disease of addiction.*

Hip Replacement at a South Shore Hospital

The Hospital

Wake up time: Dr. Siric and all his staff consulted with me hours before surgery. I had made my decision. I would allow the healthcare industry take control of my life again. My mind was at peace because they were in control and no more decisions were to be made. Now that I had gone through weeks of improving my nutrition and cleaning the alcohol out of my system, I would let the hospital staff do their job. For the time being the weight of pain was off my shoulders. I closed my eyes, smiled, and went to sleep.

I woke with a quick shock to my system. It may have been the people around me, the light, someone's voice, chemicals, or my body saying, "I am back." I opened my eyes to a hectic ICU. I had no pain from the waist down. I just felt an irritation to the arm, which turned out to be the needles feeding a saline solution and morphine into my body. I was drugged but smiling.

Hospital for two days: I opened my eyes, noting the tubes dangling from bottles of clear water and the sound of beeps from a machine near my head. Occasionally, an orderly or nurse would come and ask me if I had any pain, how was my stomach, and then take my pulse and temperature. At one point, Dr. Siric came with another doctor to tell me the operation went perfectly. It was then that I had my first glimpse of the x-ray that showed the titanium rod that connected to the socket, which was held to the bone by two screws. The rod looked just like an outdoor Christmas light post that you stick into the grass. A chill came into my body just thinking about how medicine could come so far as to insert a rod into the core tissue of a human thigh.

The doctors explained that I was being fed antibiotics and morphine. The former was to help the body accept a foreign object, and the latter to kill the pain and stop unnecessary movement. This went on for one day and slowly all tubes were removed, and I was fed oral painkiller from then on.

I was in a state of full surrender, but as I recovered, my personality worked its way back. I was suffering from light shock and showing no signs of shaking from detox; *my body was clean.* It was on the second day I realized a correlation between *no physical* pain and my desire *not to self-medicate* myself. During my last meeting before my discharge one of the doctors turned to me and said, "You are a very sick man!" I regret not asking specifically what he meant. What I discovered later is that the doctors told Martin that my spine was wrecked; no one would attempt to operate on my spine. Unfortunately, I had fought the pain with alcohol.

Goodbye to the hospital: I was to be released in the late morning after final med checks and papers were signed. But the day dragged on as the operating room and the recovery area became increasingly busy. It was obvious that the intake of patients was overwhelming the nursing staff. The pressure to discharge so they could accept incoming patient grew into a fury. This led to a breakdown in communication by the doctors and no instructions and scripts were provided to the next medical facility.

An orderly handed me some personal items in a plastic bag and read the discharge documents as I signed them. He reminded me that I would be taken by ambulance to the Parrington Place in Walpole for rehabilitation, so I should just sit back and relax. But as time dragged by and physical discomfort grew, I became insistent that meds be ordered even though patients are not allowed to leave the hospital in sedated state. The last comment from my nurse was, "I have my hands full and you are not the only patient." Shortly after, the gurney came, and I was transported to the ambulance. My discomfort was growing into pain.

The First Rehab Transitional Facility - Parrington

The system's first mistake - absolute pure pain: The ambulance drove me from the hospital directly to Parrington Rehabilitation and Care facility in Walpole. I signed the necessary forms and was sent to the ward for patients recovering from serious operations. Unless there are unusual complications, Parrington was used to empty the hospitals and free up beds.

8-29-2015: 16:42 Admission Summary: Note Text: "Patient is alert and oriented male who is admitted into 235B. Patient admitted s/p total L hip replacement on 8/26/2015. Patient has a history of alcohol and depression. Patient appears to be agitated and refusing to sign admission paperwork. Will attempt to have paperwork signed later in the evening."

Since the recovery room at the hospital had been over flowing at the time, I arrived late and before the midnight shift. I settled into the bed and the normal parade of staff came to introduce themselves: the room nurses, the floor nurse, and the staff person for my general needs.

It was during the second hour, when the floor light had been turned off, that I realized my pain medication had not been delivered nor had any sleep medication for that matter. After a few buzzes to the nurses' station, a staff person came to my bedside. I explained that the discomfort in my hip was increasing and that I needed a pain killer as soon as possible. Approximately half hour went by and the pain level was now a level six, so I called the nurses' desk repeatedly for help.

As the pain increased I lost track of time. Then the room nurse finally arrived. She explained to me that the prescriptions had not been transferred from the hospital to the facility's doctors. Since it was after hours and no one in either facility was available, no pain medication could be given. The nurse informed me that when the doctors arrived in the morning, script s could be transferred, and medication would be provided. I did the math and it hit me--that meant for two days after a total hip replacement operation, I would have NO medication of any kind, not even aspirin.

It took less than an hour before the pain reached level 8 to 9. Since I could not get out of bed without assistance, I was bedridden in agony. My first burst of screams drew no attention, and I have no clue how long it lasted. I was visited two more times by the floor nurses, and a staff person ordered me to stop screaming; "Patients can hear you down the hall!" "Then give me at least Tylenol please," I said. "No, there are no orders", the head nurse said. My plea to call the doctors was unheard, and my screams intensified. It was as if something was tearing at my hip muscles with burning finger tips.

Visions entered my mind of the books, documentaries, and movies about people being operated on without medication. This would be my third day of bone, tissue, nerves, and skin healing itself. Now I had firsthand knowledge of what, at some level, it must have been like for them.

The night nurse comes to the rescue: The nursing and staff shift changed, and the night staff came on duty. I looked up and an older nurse was standing above me holding a small cup with 2 pills and a cup of water. She smiled and asked me to take the pills. Without hesitation, the meds went down my throat as fast as a swallow would allow. "I have no comments about why things were not addressed, but I have been a nurse all my life. We must use common sense. I gave you 2 Tylenol with Codeine; that should help so you can make it until morning." The nurse and I talked about the attitude of old-school nurses who would limit the torture I was going through.

<u>8-30-2015: 05:51 Type: eMar – Medication Administration Note.</u>

"Note text: Percocet Tablet 5-325 mg. Given 2 tablet by mouth every 6 hours as needed for severe pain. PRN. Administration was effective."

It took from 8/29 - 16:42 pm to 8/30 – 5:51 am to receive pain medication. As I continue sharing my experience we can see what healthcare for the common person looks like. From this experience, I can say the top item on the patient's own check list to ask or do is for the "communication" of medication between doctors, staff, and any facility transfer. Parrington was rated a four star out of five for rehabilitation after surgery. This may teach us that a homeless person, who is alone and has no family or friends to be with them, needs an advocate provided by the healthcare system! Who else gives a damn?

Learning the Parrington System

Four-star environment: Despite the personality types you find anywhere, Parrington was rated a four-star Rehabilitation and Transitional Facility. That meant it helped and worked for those who needed physical rehabilitation from operations and those who no longer could take care of themselves in senior centers, villages, and assisted living.

Parrington was off Route 1 in Walpole, tucked next to an upscale housing development. The buildings were surrounded with trees, bushes, and flowers. As you entered the lobby, the sitting room to your left had a beautiful New England-style look and feel. The hallway throughout the building contained bedrooms, offices, dining rooms, meeting rooms, TV rooms, and rehab rooms. It was designed so well that you felt good no matter where you went; the environment was clean and happy. Wheel chairs, walker, canes, and equipment were clean and new. The bathrooms were spotless and did not smell. The atmosphere was calm.

The program: The program was simple. Two days of bed rest, and then I was scheduled for daily physical rehab. The meals were timed and wheelchair equipment was assigned if I left my room. The objective was to orientate me to a wheel chair, then the walker, and the last hurdle was the cane.

Roommates - help for those who have no hope: I had two roommates. As I lay in bed, I had Dennis to my right and Phil to my left.

Phil: Phil was an older man whose family was arranging assisted living as the next step in his life. He had been a VP of Engineering at a medium technology company. Engineers have their own language and are accustomed to analyzing. Because I am analytical by nature we got along well. It was my job to make sure his wheelchair did not run over his breathing tubes, especially when he went into the bathroom.

Dennis: Dennis was a 28-year-old man. For the first few days, I never saw Dennis's face. Dennis's space in the room was off limits to anyone other than the staff, nurses, doctors, and family. White curtains attached to the walls by clips walled off his space. It was mandatory that everyone switch into insulated gowns, gloves, booties, masks, and head gear before entering. His visitors were his family, and they had to dress in the same manner.

I only heard Dennis talking on the phone to family and friends. His activity was watching the TV and playing on a 17" laptop with all the Internet applications. It took two days for any communication between us; I broke the silence by asking him if he wanted my candy that Mike and Liz Garrison brought to me. I knew that I was not allowed near Dennis, but I could throw things at him. I guess no one had done that before. When I asked the staff why it was the way it was, they said nothing. HIPPA, the privacy safeguard of the patient in the United States, was the reason.

Rock climbing – a body cut short: By the end of the first week, Dennis and I were talking occasionally. The short conversations led to his disclosing his circumstances. At the age of 17, Dennis was rock wall climbing in a mall. He slipped and fell after climbing ¾ of the way to the top; the safety straps did not work. The fall severed part of his spine, which eliminated his ability to walk; though he could turn over and use his hands. The worst came later when he contracted MRSA, an antibiotic resistant bacterium, in the health institutions. On top of the MRSA, there were additional complications affecting his breathing and eating. Dennis will be that way for the rest of his life. *The key to his care is moving from institution to institution so the health care bills would be paid.*

We became friends enough that I could open the curtain and throw him any goodies that had been given to me or stolen by me. Dennis's job was to catch them.

The hell of learning good nurse-bad nurse: *You would think that my experience in hospitals would be at the expert level considering what happened in 2011 and the total of 7 months in 2014 and 2015. You must understand that those months were for urgent care and substance rehabilitation. For me, Parrington and facilities to come were for physical rehabilitation and to create an off the street living solution. My material about hospital is for you to feel for the people and get a good or bad understanding of the health care system.*

Unfortunately, nurses and staff are in control at these facilities; they have the responsibility and the authority to act when they see fit. If you are functioning well cognitively, sometimes their actions and attitudes could be confrontational; regardless, there is no recourse.

On the 3rd day at Parrington, there was an episode after Mike brought over 4 bags and luggage I had at his house. We figured that I was on a path that would not bring me back to the Garrison's house. While speaking to a nurse I had just met on the floor, *I made a short comment about sorting my clothes in my luggage and retrieving my meds.* Within fifteen minutes, the head nurse and staff member came to my room and asked me to sit in the hall while they ripped through my luggage. Their approach and demeanor were like pit bulls. When I asked why, they said that I had brought in illegal drugs. Twenty minutes later, they came out and said I could return to my room. I asked if they found anything. One nurse said, "No." I asked, "Did the red-haired nurse send you on this hunt?" She said, "It is unimportant." I asked if I would get an apology. She said, "No."

I became aware that I must control what I say and how I say it. But I had no clue of the future and how knowing about good nurse-bad nurse was so important.

Rehabilitation off course? The goal to get me on my feet meant working according to Parrington's plan. I was working with the wheelchair to move around the room and down the hall.

I was being given Percocet every 5 to 6 hours as well as my vitamins and my standard meds.

"9/2/2015: 14:30 pm Note text: No cough or congestion no distress. Left Hip x-ray recommended. Waiting Dr. Hallard to call back. Left hip staples intact, no signs of infection.

The following day, I was graduated to a walker with a yellow star. That meant I could only use the walker in my room and in the short hallway.

9/3/2015: 5:38 am Note text: Complaint of pain in the left hip. Medicated with good effect. Talking with patient, developed spasm to the left hip. Call to M.D. Complaint of insomnia, medicated with good effect. Call light in place, able to make needs known.

9/3/2015: 15:02 pm Note text: Dr. Hallard aware of increased redness and warmth left hip staples and small amt. of drainage. New order Keflex 1,000 mg by mouth 2 x 7 days. Acidophilus 1 tab po 2 x day x 14 day.

Something was not right. It was shortly after the hip replacement that I discovered the operation made me sick. The key words are redness, warmth/hot, drainage and pain: signs of infection.

The Beginning of Opportunities and Assets to be Used

The website begins: I had plenty of time to sit and meditate about what had transpired in the last few years. I started to compose a timeline in my mind correlating it to my homelessness and the breakdown of my body.

The words kept coming back to me repeatedly about what I said to myself in the snow of Quincy and Marlboro, "Someone should know about this." A story line started to develop of "the Brady Bunch" gone nuts, high income, homelessness, and financial devastation. That is when it hit me to call Dr. Virginia Dwyer, the wife of Bob Dwyer, a lifelong friend. Virginia worked in research at a university and had volunteered to edit my book.

> My first conversation with Virginia was not what I expected. She educated me about the preparation for a book and the use of my journals. It was her idea to start a blog to transfer my experiences and education along the way. As I listened, it made perfect sense.

First, start a website or blog to create theme. I would work with my idea to help people. *I would let them see what happened, what could happen to them, and scare them away from doing the same thing.* Virginia was well-versed in WordPress, which is used to create blogs and websites. She would set it up, and I would create the content. We set up a timeline and the website were born: www.addictionrealityeducation.com

Next Step – a place to live: Almost every day, I was texting or talking to Mike and Martin. We knew that the Parrington was a short-term rehab solution since MassHealth will only cover a specific number of days. I started calling the Serenity Center and SMAK Housing Department to find housing within Marlboro. Again, the city would have all the facilities and services I would need to get on my feet.

Parrington medical notes - "9/8/2015: 15:25 pm: Note Text: Meeting w/Brian, Case Manager and this SW. RT continues to complain of some discomfort and has not completed stairs. Also, he is homeless and has been for some time with intermittent employment. Staff explained to Brian that his insurance benefit may reimburse to keep him here until he can do stairs or feels he is able to d/c. Brian working with SMAK and some outside housing authorities, but housing may not be available before his benefits are cut. Explained to Brian that the Business Office will approach him at this point r/t paying for room and board if he does not have d/c plans. SW to assist as needed. Author: Social Services Specialist (e-SIGNED)"

"9/9/2015: 4:43 am: Note Text: Alert and oriented. DX; necrosis of the left hip/left hip replacement. Complaint of pain to left hip, *medicated with good effect.* Complaint of spasm, medicated with good effect. Dressing intact to left hip. Complaint of insomnia, *medicated with good effect.* Author: Nurse"

"9/10/2015: 01:28 am: Note Text: Complaint of pain to L hip, medicated with good effect. Complaint of spasm to L hip, medicated with good effect. Steri strips in place to left hip. Continues on Keflex for L hip incision infection. Temp 99.3. Wheelchair for long distances. Author: NP nurse."

After twelve days of hospital/nursing home rehabilitation, I was still experiencing pain and spasms in the left hip. I assumed it was normal considering the seriousness of the operation. The real issue was that after nearly two weeks, Percocet and Trazodone were still needed for the medical team to write, "medicated with good effect." I was running out of time with nowhere to go. After my conversations with Mike and Martin, I realized the Garrison's house was not an option for me, and Martin's house was not either. What to do for housing with pain that persists?

The first important changes, booze or no booze: For me, the rehab facility was paradise. Other than a few bad nurses, the employees were helpful, understanding, accommodating, and friendly: all smiles. It was my chance to block out the memories of the street, the shelters, the sober houses, the hospitals, and the street culture. The drugs masked the pain, so my head had time to clear. Without realizing it, I was coming upon 30 days without alcohol. My mood was better, and my motivation to get my legs working was high. I could not wait to move to cane training.

Another episode happened when I had learned that the kitchen closed at 7:30. After that, only small soda, water, and snacks were available. It did not take me long to "walker" up to the nurse's station with a smile on my face and my gift of the Irish Blarney to win over the nurses' stations staff. It was at the end of the second week. After making it to the circular nurse's station, I stood and noticed an empty area. Since it was circular, you could see what was on the desks. To my amazement, there, right at arm's length, was a bottle of vodka. With fast hands, I could grab it and walk, but I did not do it. When the nurses came back, I put in my order and asked about the Vodka. I was floored at the response. "Look, there are men and woman here until they edge into dementia. They deserve respect and some enjoyments. So, the staff or maintenance will bring in the stuff. It is against the rules but right is right. You okay"? I had the chance, but I turned it down. Before I left Parrington, I had multiple chances to steal or order the vodka, but I did not.

That event sparked the realization that there can be change, and I was changing.

Miracles Can Happen - Revelations and Actions Taken

A letter came about my past: At the beginning of the second week Mike Garrison brought my mail and my normal allotment of candy. One of the letters was from Westborough Moving and Storage, which had my beds, lamps, desks, clothes, personal keepsakes, photos, and Johnny's childhood knickknacks from birth to his senior year in high school. It was a bill for $10,000 and a letter regarding time payments. So much had happened since the moving and storage company had taken my possessions, I had forgotten about them.

That day, I received a call from Howie Rubin, Sal's son, who graduated from law school and was working in the family business.

I started the conversation:

"Howie - thank you for calling. I received the bill for $10,000 for the bins I have rented over the years. I had thought I would be back working by this time and would have paid you in full. Howie, I am still in a hospital and to pay you anything is not reality. I would like to offer you all my furniture and property which you may be able resell at a reasonable price. Everything else of no value to you, I give you my permission to put in your trash dumpster."

Howie Rubin's response:

"Brian, we know what you have gone through and heard of events when you lived in town. We are not a company that just forecloses on our customers in hard times. Why don't you have your friends and family come and take what is important from the three storage bins and we will dispose of the rest? I will draft a one-page agreement. Should you get well, we can pay down the balance of what remains after your family leaves- the estimated value, if there is any."

Short of falling out of bed, I held back my tears to finish the negotiation. "Howie, that sounds fantastic," I said. "I do not know what to say, but God made good men, and you and your father are two of those." An agreement was written, and timelines were set. Timelines which depended upon me getting my people to the storage bins.

A call to Jane and Greg Sellers: That same day, I made the call to Jane. I explained the offer from the Rubin's and asked if she and Greg were willing to repeat what they had done in 2013 before I moved out of my apartment and hit the street. It was a miracle or "Chi" in the air because Jane and Greg had been discussing coming to Massachusetts and seeing me. Their family activities had slowed down, so there was free time in the month of September.

Jane and Greg would rent a U-Haul in Westborough and drive it over to the storage bins. Howie would have his men empty the three bins and lay all the contents on the floor. Jane and Greg would select the items to take back to Skaneateles for safe keeping.

Anything remaining would be given to the moving and storage company to reduce my bill, or else given to charity.

This coincidence of lucky breaks helped me take a step toward normalcy. One of the significant debts hanging over my head would be minimized and control of my very important personal items that held decades of memories would be saved. I had given up *hope* to save the past. Good fortune and the kindness of others started a move in the right direction, as if something or someone was creating a good path.

Martin's secret plan: The 11th to the 15th of the month were typical days. One afternoon I received a call from Martin, but I ignored it due to the blood tests they were doing. Then the phone would ring again. Martin was calling repeatedly until I picked up. "Brian, where have you been? I have been calling and you did not answer. Hell, you're only in one spot, are you okay? Look, I have spoken with June who runs a house for SMAK in Marlboro. Do not ask for details but she needs your information *by 5 pm today*. Her organization needs the information to review whether your history can justify housing. She needs a timeline of your homelessness. Do not hold back a thing. Can you do it?"

I had two hours to send the email to her.

This is where the real tragedy came to light. It was just one of many that you will meet in a short time. By understanding this service provided by an organization and the process I followed, you too may cut short your learning curve of homelessness.

From: Brian   masters
Sent: Monday,   September   7,   2015   9:58   AM
To: xxxx@smak.org;   xxxx@smak.com
Cc: brianmasters919@gmail.com;   brian   masters
Subject: Homeless Time Line for brian masters

June;

I have outlined the moves I had to take to have a roof over my head, have a sober environment and be safe.

DATES, NOTES AND DESCRIPTIONS

Aug. 26th to present

A Hospital hip operation and recovery.
When released, I have nowhere to go.

Aug.14th to Aug. 26th

Stayed with friends, Mike and Liz Garrison in Canton, Ma

July 27th to Aug.14th

Longwood Hospital, pre-operation physical therapy.

February 7th to July 27th

Stayed at the Burger Hotel in Marlboro
One room with no internet. 58 stairs. Unsafe: drugs, alcohol,
fights and stealing.

Jan. 22nd to Feb. 7th

Mike and Liz Garrison in Canton Ma.

Jan. 20th to Jan 22nd

I slept in my car.

Jan. 7th to Jan. 20th.

I stayed at a shelter in Quincy. I was mugged the first night
for my suitcase. Police came in the nick of time. At the shelter I
developed pneumonia and was hospitalized.

January 5th to January 7th

I stayed with Mike and Liz in Canton, MA

Dec. 28th, 2014 to January 5th, 2015

I went to Upstate NY to stay with family and friends.

Dec. 25th, 2014 to December 28th

I lived in my car.

Nov. 27th, 2014 to Dec. 24th

I lived at Mike and Liz Garrison's in Canton Ma

Nov. 26th to Nov. 27th, 2014

I drove to Westboro and lived in my car, which broke down in the nor'easter. Westboro Police arrived and helped me out. I have a good reputation.

Nov. 14th, 2014 to. 26th 2014

I lived at the Worcester shelter. I was holding down two jobs at security and Macy's. Then I was robbed and pistol whipped for items in my car. I left Worcester asap,

Nov. 11th, 2014 to Nov. Nov. 14th, 2014

I lived in my car.

Sept. 3rd, 2014 to Nov. 10th

I stayed at the Palladin House in Marlboro MA
I was holding down two jobs.

Aug. 25th, 2014 to Sept. 3rd

I stayed at my karate instructor's house.

Aug. 23rd to Aug. 25th, 2014

Slept in the car.

July 31st, 2014 to Aug. 23rd, 2014

Bishop's shelter in Waltham on Lexington Street.

June 30th, 2014 to July 31st, 2014

Davis Rehabilitation in Dorchester, while staying at
Mike's sober house in JP.

June 28th, 2014 to July 31st, 2014

I committed myself to Pembroke to understand depression and drinking.

The email was sent by 4:30 the same day. I emailed copies to myself and Martin. Martin was a calm executive who managed dozens of sales people nationwide; he was always under control, but not this time. I did what I was told to do. At the end of the day, I still did not know why I had to send it ASAP and what it was specifically for. That mystery would start to be solved in two months; a full discovery came within the next year.

More good fortune - A corporation that understands the homeless: One morning in September Jane and Greg arrived at Westborough Moving and Storage. The workers had laid out all my property from the three bins on the floor of the warehouse as Howie had promised. By the end of it all, the workers helped pack the U-Haul and Jane and Greg were on the way to Walpole to meet me.

I had been very excited to see them after all this time, true family at last. While I was getting up and dressed to meet them, there was an increased pain in the left hip. So much so, that I had to revert to my wheelchair.

I looked pale and in pain, but seeing their faces provided a needed boost. We had a great time talking; there was no stigma. I was also sober, which was a big improvement over the last time they saw me. Mike arrived, amazed that I was back in the wheelchair, but ready to see them again and transfer my TV to his car; a gift for helping me. The downer was when the nurse came out to give me my pills and a shot in the stomach. Of course, this brought out a conversation about the meds I had to take, for how long, and next steps. The table became strangely quiet *when Mike and I had no answer to these questions*. We stared into each other's eyes, the table, the trees, and our hands. It was very weird in a way.

We all said our goodbyes and gave hugs accompanied by mild teary eyes. Mike was on his way to Canton and Jane and Greg were driving all the way back to Skaneateles. It was a five-hour trip down the Mass Pike, over the Berkshires, past Albany, over the boring flat road through Utica and Syracuse until they reached the Finger Lakes exit, the exit that would make them happy.

The last of my possessions were safe but after all the excitement had worn off, it was time to face the obvious. Why was I back in a wheelchair with pills for the pain, and *where and when do I go from here?*

Health System and Insurance – Money as Always

Social Services calls me in: I had been working on the website and taking notes for its future content when Alicia, the head of Social Services came to my table in the patient's TV and internet lounge with clipboard in hand. "Mr. Masters, we need to talk about your end of stay at Parrington," she said. I knew the tone of voice quite well. It was the tone of business that I had lived with since I left college. Alicia was all business. She explained to me that the basic health plan covered only two to three weeks of rehabilitation and medication. At the end of that period, a patient must return to his previous residence to live. She noticed in the notes that I was homeless. She asked if I could stay at Mike's or Martin's. My answer was, "No." "Then we have a problem," Alicia stated. "Business is business, Mr. Masters, and that is what we run. I do not like to be the heavy, but Parrington is not a hotel or a shelter. You need to figure out a solution, Brian."

It was time to face reality. I knew that I had to go, and the shelter and houses had plenty of men and women using canes and even walkers. My friend Fred at the Worcester hellhole shelter used crutches. Yet, it was hard for me to imagine going back to the subculture, especially the way I was. I would be a sitting duck for abuse. Opening my mouth would be a sign for them to "come and get me." Plus, I had been alcohol-free for five weeks. Going back to the shelters would be a disaster. I had come too far to slide back now and give up.

Regression of my health does not stop the system: 9/16/2015: 01:05 "Ambulating with a walker to the bathroom. Patient out of the room in the wheelchair self-propelling on the unit. Percocet given as ordered with effect. Steri strips intact on the left hip."

Now my ability to walk started to become impaired. Just the day before, I had been moving around my floor with the cane. But while walking to the nurse's station I had to grab the handrail in the hallway, so I did not fall. With the cane in hand, a "new" sharp pain in the left hip area raced through me. The pain was so unpredictable that I needed to retreat to a wheelchair to make my appointment and maintain my routine. Something was not right. I made sure the head nurse knew and I asked to see the doctor.

9/17/2015: "C/O L hip pain 5/10. Med with 23 Percocet at 7:45. Resting comfortably at this time."

I had been naive in 2011 after the spine operation, and as I look back, I was naive after the hip operation- not as much, but still naive. Now, just a little after three weeks since the operation, I was having intermittent spikes of pain in the hip and groin. I should have been all over that doctor's ass. Where was the doctor?

On 9/19, I had severe pain. The nurses gave me my sixth hour Percocet's and I used my wheelchair to go back to physical therapy. When I came through the door, the manager on duty informed me that my therapy was complete and there would be no more sessions. "Your insurance ran out, Brian."

"MassHealth will no longer pay for your sessions," the therapist informed me. "There is nothing we can do." I thanked her, turned the chair around and wheeled down the hall to try the walker or cane again.

Time to Leave Parrington

Called to the Director's office: Journal, 9-20: On morning of September 20th, I was called to the Director's office for meeting about a next move. This time I walked to the office with my cane since I just had my dose of Percocet. I was determined to look my best.

Alice came out of her office to greet me with a smile. We sat down and faced each other. I can only describe it as a sales call where you are going to meet with the decision maker to hear whether you won or lost the deal. "Well Brian, you have gone through a lot. My staff has provided all good reports, complemented with good things to say about your motivation. We know you have nowhere to go, and it may not be your fault. We also agreed that you are still having issues with the left hip and your back. I have contacted a sister facility and sent your files and my recommendation. If you agree, we can send you there. They can sort out the left hip pain, dietary issues, and *right* leg weakness. Brian, this will provide a roof over your head and the time to sort things out. What do you think?"

I cannot say that the feeling was like winning and closing a million-dollar deal, but it was close! I thanked her for meeting with me and telling me the news. I then complimented her staff and the way things were run. "If I get back on my feet, I will try to reciprocate."

I also said, "Alice, where am I going to in your healthcare chain?

Alice responded, "Westborough. It is an older facility but was acceptable to MassHealth. A van will be here in the morning to take you there. Do you know where Westborough is?"

My response was, "Yes I do. Thank you."

Mike, Martin, and my friends were no longer viable financial supports. Yes, I was still in medical facilities, which provided a roof over my head and continued sobriety, but I still had serious physical *medical issues. **If I had been out on the street, I would not have made it!** With only six weeks of sobriety, and I still had pain that only opiates could stop. I could have hidden it for a short time on the street, but illegally.*

Memories of my life in Westborough flooded my mind. My stay in the town I had called home for twenty-four years would be three months and fifteen days. It gave me the time and resources to make plans, and they were life changing.

I will shorten my account of the Westborough institutionalization with a condensed timeline. I will walk you through the health system and federal government action as part of my experience. We will meet the real people, events, and environments which led to multiple discoveries.

Step by Step: Back to the Boro's Brings Hope

Setting the Foundation Paths for Recovery

A true nursing home: The van drove 495 north toward New Hampshire, and I knew exactly where we would take the exit. My mind had a quick daydream of taking the van and driving up to Lake Winnipesaukee, using my remaining money for a cheap cabin, getting a job, and just living. The dream was short lived as I noticed we passed the Mass Pike sign and were squealing around the corner of the exit. As we took a left off Main Street to the end of the cul-de-sac, I recognized the building. I had passed by this short street and the Regatta Deli many times, but I never recognized the building at the end for the street; it was a skilled nursing facility.

"My God", I said to myself. "This is the building where I stayed during my last rehab in 2011. This is where I learned to walk and talk enough to fool the doctors and staff to release me to my house in Westborough. I had been labeled highly infectious for a time. I had to crawl and sneak to the nurse's station to get juice. They must have really messed me up if I've forgotten this place." Now I was back.

My memories came back as I entered the building. The glass windows on the right separated the administration from the hall and the patients. You could see two offices in the back for the Director and another manager. There were no frills in this place.

What Westborough Transitional Care was not: The administrator signed the papers and gave them back to the driver of the van. The administrator smiled and welcomed me.

The elevator had reached the third floor when I realized I had been on the second floor in 2011. I was wheeled down the hall, passing rooms with numbers on them. Each room was almost the same. The nurses' station was in the middle of the floor. The internal area of the floor consisted of the food elevator, the main elevator, closets, two more offices, supply rooms, and a meds storage cart with heavy metal locks.

What the floor was not:

- Lined with flowery wall paper

- Built with firm smooth flooring matching the color of the walls

- Designed so the nurses' station was easily accessible

- Empty of the med carts, soiled clothes bins, and lab equipment

What the floor was:

- Decorated with lime-colored walls and painted metal trim

- Designed so each room was rectangular to accommodate four beds

- Equipped with standard hospital beds with limited comfort controls

- Rooms without TVs

- Meal tables on wheels and small personal hospital chests for each bed

- Smelling of meds, shit, and piss masked by perfume

- Room to room, shared bathrooms

- Halls filled with walkers, med carts, wheelchairs and patients sitting or walking

My room was 6D, six for the room, D for being the fourth bed in the room. On the left was bed A for Jim and B for Tom. Bed C was on the right for Sam and bed D for me; I was near the window.

I kept reminding myself that I had a roof over my head and a clean bed. I had to realize that the nursing home environment was "the only game in town" for me. I knew I must *ride the wave and live with it or go back to the street and lose it all together.*

What Westborough Transitional Care was: Now that I made up my mind to survive in this facility, I could take the new next steps. I needed to learn to exist in my surroundings. The transitional facility was keeping me out of the subculture. Fortunately, it was not like any of the institutions, housing, or shelters I had been in before. WTC was a nursing home. Most people in life, especially at my age, visit these places but never actually live in one.

WTC provided the food, shelter, and a staff. That meant the patients could focus on what was important to them, whether it was healing from an operation, time to diagnosis a problem, or endure the next deterioration of the brain.

As we move forward, I will attempt to be brutally honest about the events, people and environment. It is not the street culture where food and shelter are an everyday struggle. Here life's events started to come together, enabling me to beat the disease and regain a life.

As the body repairs itself, new plans and expectations are needed: No one had given me any idea or plan of the future. I was assigned a room, a doctor, roommates, and a floor; "Here you are Brian, go for it." So, I did what I knew best. I kept my mind busy and organized some semblance of a plan.

* Get working on the internet blogs and stay focused

* Work with Martin and Mike for permanent housing

* Determine the true status of my health

* Stay in touch with far away friends and family - support

Note the fact that jobs, money, and cars are not in the plan. Health - what my body and mind could take moving forward- were now important. I had literally survived due to texts and occasional emails from Jim Goodman, the Foxes, Jack and Beth, Jane and Greg, and James and Clare.

Drinking, partying, and my selfish drive were being replaced by a need to discover "why?" Why the pain, loss of control, and inability to stop? What did the contributors do in five years that four decades of living had not?

The People Who Kept Me Focused

The nursing home is a world unto itself. In this world I discovered who I was now and who I did not want to be. My time at the WTC taught me that although it was not a shelter, WTC had many similarities, which meant I needed to fall back techniques for physical and mental survival. Clearly, there are those who will move on and those who will be "lifers." My goal was to further myself.

Roommates: The first roommate I came across was Jim. Jim screamed on and off throughout the first night. He would scream just for attention; it was hell every day. Jim was placed on the third floor because he was not yet ready for the first floor, which is the memory care floor. Plus, people with dementia could not take his yelling and disruption.

The second roommate was Tom. He was a retired engineer from the computer revolution era. Jim had been at the facility short of a year. He would go to Worcester Hospital off and on for tests. Tom would constantly tell Jim to shut up; sometimes it worked, and sometimes it did not. Man, did he welcome me there. We became good friends until the day he died in his bed.

The third roommate was Sam. Sam was admitted for depression, and as time went on, it became apparent he had been extremely violent and was currently heavily sedated. Sam and I spoke maybe a total of one hour over the whole three and a half months I was there.

The Doctor: Dr. G was an experienced clinician. She came from Venezuela, studied in the United States, and always had a serious look on her face. At first, Dr. G did not have much respect for my feedback after she had reviewed my records.

Intake notes from Doctor G, taken 9-19-2015:

- Left hip replacement; taped and sterile; cannot walk

- Anomia

- Abnormal in view of ETOH use at last 2011

- ETOH – not drinking for greater than 1 month

- Anxiety

In other words, I was sick and she had a report of substance use but no history to understand why; her attitude was pure stigma. It took more than month to change Dr. G's opinion of me, but the effort would be well worth the attempt. Now I had an intellectual challenge: a doctor with an attitude who would have to work with me whether she liked it or not.

The Housing Director – Amy: Amy was 4'11", bleach blonde. We clashed at first. I felt that her approach to housing for street people was elementary and she thought that I was full of myself. We were both right. We became friends and remained so until the day she was let go; I never found out why, but the rumor was budget cuts.

One day I told Amy some of what I had experienced in the last year. It was then she told me her **true** story. Not more than three years before, she and her two children were on the streets outside of Springfield. They were fortunate because they had made a home inside a car in a junkyard. Amy came up with the idea of getting a steak, which she fed to the "junk yard dog." At first, they had to run to the car. As time went on, the dog expected the steak and let them take their time and finally ignored them. With the car as their home, Amy got some part-time jobs. Then she used her real resume and reinvented herself with her knowledge about housing for the poor. Her job pulled in $65,000, her kids were in school, and the physically abusive husband was gone forever. There was no doubt about the truth of her story. I could see it in her eyes. Amy and the kids were survivors.

Think about it. Out of the blue, I come across a person, with children, who made my street existence look like an easy street. As I said wrote in the preface, some people have been there and want to help. Also, try walking in her shoes.

Day by day. Month by Month. Positive Paths are Offered

Within a short period of time, it became apparent that WTC was a new path. It was not a detox center or a badly designed commitment facility like Pembrook. The patients were sick but they were "normally" sick. They were old but "normally" old. The doctor, directors, and the staff were there for the long run and did NOT expect to have their patients rotated every five days or two weeks. Unknown to me, the time I spent at WTC positioned me for a total "reset." With the help of Martin Philips, I had new ideas for next moves. With the help of selected patients and staff, I experienced normalcy. The time at WTC set the foundation for my will power and made me aware of solutions which could save other lives as well as my own.

Positive Paths Begin

Social Security Disability – financial stability: During the last week of September, Martin came to visit. Of course, being my mentor and always focused on planning, he made a comment about Social Security Disability Insurance. "Considering the infection of 2011 and the disintegration of your hip and legs, you should be an ideal candidate," Martin said. That comment from Martin stuck in my head. In 2012, when I was recovering from the spinal infection, SSDI was not an opinion since my estate still had roughly $80,000. Now, in 2015, the combination of the spine, hip and leg complications, the fact I had no money, and the dim prospects for a good future job made me willing to apply.

I will walk through the process of applying, preparing, interviewing, and receiving SSDI. Many individuals truly require help. Careful work and preparation is essential to winning your case. I hope you will learn something from it.

Whether filling online or on paper, the following are required for a chance at success. In my opinion:

- A primary physician who will agree

- Detailed hospital records of the disability

- Detailed surgeons' records and credible medical staff records and reports

- Appointments with a federal/state approved psychiatrist and medical doctors who are not your doctors.

The forms state that if you are turned down the first time, you have the right to reapply within a certain time period.

My first step was to retrieve the 2011 operation records. I called each surgeon's office and hospital for release forms and records to be sent to either Mike's house or WTC. Over a period of one month, the documents arrived from the attending surgeon's office and all the hospitals. It was my job to put together my case.

Martin Phillips took on the challenge of organization and making my claim successful. He was able the take the records, copy them, and give them to me. I was then able to put them in order chronologically. I had plenty of free time, so reading, highlighting, and taking notes was easy.

At this time, additional pain developed in the spine and the new hip. To control these episodes, the nurses provided me with my allotted Percocet's. Blood tests indicated that my liver was negatively affected by the Percocet's. The Percocet's were replaced with Oxycodone.

The reports tell the real damage 2011 did: Martin and I each made copies of four sets of records. The four sets covered the pre-diagnosis, the first operation, admittance for an infection from the operation, and the timeline of records and nurse's notes of everything that had transpired.

It is hard to explain my feeling as I read and reread those documents. I could not understand the codes and numbers that were used. But the detail in plain English was amazing:

• Second operation, the removal of bone fragments from the first operation

• The steril pads being place on the new stitches after reopening the spine section L-4 and L-5.

• Controls needed so as not to damage the nerves.

• The failing of the renal part of the body

• The advance of failure into the respiratory system

• Induce brain and heart activity prognosis.

• Removal of small bone fragments in the third operation

On and on, each time I read the records and highlighted the sentences, I was amazed at how remarkable it all was, and how the body could be so sensitive and beautiful in the way it worked to survive.

I organized and highlighted, while Martin acted as my legs and financier for making copies and delivering them back to me. Not only did I have my copy, but I made three other sets for the investigators and their process. I estimated the number of pages to be over 100 in each set.

The SSDI investigation: During the second month Mike delivered a letter from SSDI stating that I would be required to meet with a physician and a psychiatrist separately. I would be receiving the notice of appointment dates shortly. This meant that I had made the first preliminary cut in the approval process. Now it was time to make sure the sets of records were complete and ready to come with me on the appointments.

The first appointment- physical damage was with Doctor Mark who had graduated from Harvard Medical School and was now employed by the government. I waited in the lobby while Dr. Mark finished with a previous appointment. Since the office door was open, I heard the end of the conversation. The applicant hoped that the doctor would approve her. The money was very important to her and the family. Her inability to walk and stand for a period of time limited her, she told him. The Doctor responded, "I will read the final statements from your doctors and you will be contacted by mail."

Now it was my turn. I noticed that not only was it a small office, but dull and somewhat messy. The certificates on the wall were impressive and deserved respect. As Martin and I discussed, these doctors have seen all kinds of applicants with all sorts of stories. Dr. Mark would be ready for anything. He asked me to briefly explain my background and circumstance, which I tried to do. But my explanation was too much for him to take in. Partly through the conversation, I suggested he read the highlighted records. As he scanned the first five to ten pages, he stopped. "Mr. Masters, may I have a copy of this? I promise to shred it when I am done." My comment back to him was, "That is your copy!" During our one-hour meeting Dr. Mark again asked if he could take the highlighted records back to Cambridge. He again promised to shred them. I said yes, we shook hands, and he said I would be having one more appointment and then a decision would come in the mail. The first appointment was done.

The second appointment – mental damage came two weeks later. Dr. Gail was a psychiatrist. During the hour-long meeting I told her about the divorce, the attack, and the details of the operation. I gave her a copy of the reports and explained their content. She then gave me a memory test. She would repeat words, then more words, and then I had to repeat them. I never got it right. The doctor also asked questions about what I would do in various hypothetical situations. When the appointment ended, Dr. Gail restated what Dr. Mark had said about notification.

My SSDI investigation stage was over in November, the second full month of my stay at WTC.

My stay was three and a half months, and each day would merge into the other without excitement or meaning. I will explain my life in the facility by the people I met and our interactions. The WTC was nothing like the institutions I or my street culture friends were used to. Fate had reached out its hand again to put a roof over my head, not on the street or in a wet shelter during the coldest months of the year. Yet, I was not medically fit to go back on the street. You will experience the true people in a nursing home that provides rehabilitation for those who cannot afford better care. With a place to stay and time, I came up with action plans to give me a fighting chance at defeating the disease.

I Realize Major Changes and the Glimmer of Hope

Abstinence repairs the brain: After being pulled out of the Burger Hotel, a stay Mike and Liz's house, and then the operation, I had been sober for over two months. I noted a change one day was when I was watching TV, seeing programs of happy and sad life events. Even though my body was clean and repairing itself, my mind still would drift off and create "What would I do" scenarios. For example, if a TV program had a good ending, I would think to myself, "We will all go into Boston for drinks and celebrate!"

I had watched a TV program like that one day in November. In the past this program <u>would have triggered</u> the daydream of partying with friends. I was on the elevator going to the third floor when I realized my mind *had not drifted to any such daydream* in over a week. As the next few weeks went by, the temptations seemed to have left me. It was then I recalled my "commitment learning" from the Davis facility and their Ph.D.s, the Yale Study, and the 90-day effect. My reasoning ability may have been repaired or something else may have happened, but it was as clear as day--*<u>I had changed.</u>*

It was a fact that I could slip out at dusk and walk the quarter-mile to the liquor store without detection, but I never did. Money was not an issue since I had some money in the bank. No one would suspect Brian Masters of doing such a thing, yet I never had the craving or desire.

The right leg pain is correctly addressed: *Working with Dr. G set my life on a course of controlling pain and focusing on physical quality of life. Let's face it. Everything before 2012 was gone, my son was 3000 miles away, and it was only a matter of time before those supporting me would have to go back to their own lives. Dr. G and I had a common project, the discovery of pain management for the spine and legs. For a month, blood tests were taken regularly, and ambulances would take me for painful nerve testing at MetroWest UMass.*

A key to *the years of pain in the right leg* came from outside my task group:

• Mike had been insisting that I use a drug called Gabapentin, which had helped our friend Alice. Since I was diagnosed with neuropathy, Gabapentin would mask the pain and limit the numbing affect from the 2011 scar tissue that was touching the nerve canals.

- At the same time, Dr. Virginia Dwyer, while working with me on the website rollout, came across the clinical research of Dr. Barbara Mason on Gabapentin's effect on alcohol dependency.

- Dr. G listened. We started playing with measured doses of Gaba and Oxy for the spine and right leg. Our partnership, in the end, developed into friendship and respect.

A pattern was starting to develop. Pieces to a "path" had been revealed since leaving Pembrook. It was not clear to me at that time, but the foundation of the "Beachhead to Recovery" was being set.

Gabapentin: Gabapentin had been chosen by Dr. G and me to address the pain and numbness in the right leg. Dr. G and I slowly increased the dosage to see any significant effect. By 1200 mg per day, my symptoms started to be relieved. The pain in the spine was there but the sharp, knife-like pains that drove me to cry, scream, and drink at the Burger Hotel and Mike's house were diminishing.

Then came Dr. Virginia Dwyer's input. While working on the posts for the Addiction-Reality-Education website and our occasional conversations, we discussed Gabapentin. Virginia, being a Ph.D., researcher, and author, searched for information about the drug. She discovered a study done by Dr. Barbara Mason and the Scrip Medical Organization in California. What they found follows:

"Conclusions and relevance: Gabapentin (particularly the 1800-mg dosage) was effective in treating alcohol dependence and relapse-related symptoms of insomnia, dysphoria and craving, with a favorable safety profile. Increased implementation of pharmacological treatment of alcohol dependence in primary care may be a major benefit of Gabapentin as a treatment option for alcohol dependence."

I do fully believe that things happen for a reason. The stay at the WTC gave me the time to stay out of the cold and shelters. It was a short period of time with the support of friends and professional people. I had my cognitive reasoning ability back, a financial plan, and successful pain management. I was on the brink of learning to control the health care system instead of it controlling me.

These would be only four of the discoveries I would come upon and that I fully believe led to a positive physical and mental change. The hell of the street was still a possibility, but working the system was a precursor to my next, and hopefully last, stint at street culture existence.

Transitional Housing Becomes a Reality

The call from June and the drive with Martin: It was the first week of December and I had just returned from sending my blog to Virginia for editing when I noticed that I had a call on my cell phone. The caller ID said, "SMAK – June D." It was not until I listened to the message that I realize it was the woman to whom I had emailed the history of my homelessness.

The voicemail said, "Mr. Masters, I wanted to call you and let you know you have been approved by the state of Massachusetts for a year's grant toward no cost housing. You will be receiving a confirmation letter in the mail, but I would like to arrange a screening interview and review of the lease as soon as possible. My number is on your phone ID. Thank you, June." The word shock does not begin to describe my feeling. It was as if I closed another million-dollar computer deal that I had forgotten about.

Then I realized what had happened: "Martin!" I did the work, but Martin had made the connection. My first phone call was to him. Whether June had already told him in advance or not, he seemed surprised and happy. My next call was to June, and I suggested sometimes Martin and I could drive the five miles to Marlboro for the meeting and sign of the lease. We set the date for December 10th with an immediate move-in date.

This is a must: The day before my meeting, Martin texted me a reminder to wear my good sweater and khakis. "You want to look good and not from the street, even though you are, LOL." As an executive's mentor, Martin was always thinking of the importance of a first impression to the people who sat on the other side of the desk. Even when he drove me to follow up appointments with Dr. Siric, he insisted that I dress the part. He was driving, and he was right.

It sounds old fashioned. Whether you are on the street or coming from an institution, if you have respectable clothes or can get your hands on some, wear them. A first impression could make the difference in allowing you to begin the process to recovery/normalcy.

We turned right onto Grant Street past a 7-11 and houses that were built in before WWII. The address was 1116 Grant Street, which seemed appropriate for the housing grant I was awarded. June was an older, fragile-looking woman with a smoker's voice and no-nonsense attitude. These were her houses and the tenants lived by her rules or they were out. She smiled as she told me of the grant, and she expressed sympathy for the time I had been out on the street. The rules were simple:

- The boarding house was a drug free place

- No fighting or disturbance

- No stealing

- No overnight guests

- Notify June or her management, in writing, if you are expected to be out of the house overnight. A permission sheet had to be authorized

- Chores are assigned weekly

- Normally the cost is $85 per week but because of my hardship, I had a room at no cost for one year.

This was a SMAK transitional house. It wasn't a shelter like the Palladin House but the next step up. It was ironic. This was the house I was months away from getting into by holding down the two jobs while at the Palladin House, just before the male prostitutes set me up to get kicked out. It took just about a year to get where I was going but not much of a job--a whole year lost. I set that aside, signed the lease, and surveyed the room.

June's hesitation – As we were walking up the stairs to the second floor, June saw my weak climb up the stairs and noticed my left leg seemed painful. Before Martin and I left, she questioned whether I should have handicap devices or move to another house. We assured her that it was just a bad day, and everything was fine. Whether she bought it or not, I will never know.

There was something wrong with the replacement hip. The pain would come and go, but when it came, it was a bitch. I could walk if I extended the left leg straight out to the side, so the prosthesis would not move. But this place was my chance. I put all the past hell I experienced in Marlboro aside and went back to Westborough.

My Stay at the WTC Comes to an End

The insurance hammer comes down: Two days later, I was asked to come to the Facility Director's office for a meeting with the Director of Housing and Benefits who was present to give me the news. My insurance would only pay up to January 16th. Even though I had ongoing medical issues, my time was up and there was nothing they could do. I told them I understood and would arrange something with my family.

Whether or not you not believe in a higher power, God, or coincidence, I sure believed. I now called it, "the path," and I was going to follow it without resistance. June's house was my business, not theirs, and the holiday was two weeks away. It was then I knew my mind had changed. Maybe it was my attitude, but there was no desire for the old life. Yes, I was in pain, but Dr. G and I had started to manage the spine and neuropathy pain. My desire to party for depression, pain, or good old times drained away. That is the only way I can put it.

Holidays come and go: Christmas week was the worst for me. The left leg groin area felt like a knife was stuck in it. The pain subsided after three days, but I was done with the, "I do not see any signs of an infection in these x-rays, Mr. Masters," diagnosis coming from the hip surgeon. On top of that, I reached out to the family, and we all had conversations and wished each other a Merry Christmas. I was not sure who meant it and who did not. The tone of some voices smacked of "stigma." It could have been worse; they could have shunned me like my old business friends or a couple of so-called close friends and family.

I spoke with Johnny but things were the same. Dave Patel returned my call but I talked too much and complained. I received one card from Jane and Greg. It is extremely important to remember that these people chose to talk to me and continued to support me; I had to look at the bright side.

On January 2nd I broke the news to my friends at WTC that I was leaving. Many were glad when I initially told them, but as the days came closer to my leaving, the conversations became shorter and less confidential; we spoke about the people who passed while I was there. They were hurting, and would miss me. I did love those people.

Discharge Report:

"Date: 1-5-16: The reason for discharge: Your health has improved sufficiently so that you no longer need the services provided by the facility.

Date: 1-6-16: Doctors Report: Symptoms improving on Gabapentin. He is on 600mg/day. He has some sleepiness, but he is taking 500 mg at night. Exam same as last visit.

- Continue gabapentin.

- Continue PT and exercises at home to strengthen

- f/u in 3 months, Dr. G. 1-6-16

The facts were that I had not had PT for 2 months because insurance ran out, I was taking 1200mg/day of Gabapentin, and there would be no follow up because I needed a primary doctor once I left the facility.

Mike, Martin, and I hit the road: It was like a sequel. I packed the stuff and the guys came to pick me up, drive me to Grant Street, and help set up my new surroundings. There was no fanfare when I left, just pleasant handshakes and wishing everyone well.

As we drove into the parking lot of 1116 Grant Street, I was ready to take on what I needed for full recovery. This would be the start of finding out what I had been looking for in June 2014, when I told Mike at the motel, "I needed to know."

This part of the path would be 180 degrees different from those I had experienced before.

The First Transitional House – A Highway of Paths Discovered

The First Important Test being in The Real World

I had been out of the real world for almost five months, with most everything being done for me. Moving into the house and fending for myself meant coming back into the old reality with a new outlook. Many changes had happened mentally, which I had yet to fully understand or test. These changes renewed a strength in me.

Plan: It was the second week. I lay in *my single bed* of *my own room* and reminisced. It was just *twelve months* since I had been at Mike and Liz's house recovering from pneumonia after the Quincy shelter. It was *eleven months* since I had moved into the Burger Hotel with its numerous debaucheries. It had been only one year and so much had happened; it was almost surreal.

Then I realized it had been two years since I created a three-phase plan. I was thinking and making decisions. I possessed a new desire to help myself and justify all the work and trust others had put into me.

I was so focused that I had Mike bring back me one of the business whiteboards I had hung on my office wall along with any briefcases, documents, and tools that could help me organize. With the Plan Ahead calendar I purchased at Staples, I immediately set appointments and a schedule to get things started. Fortunately, I outlined three categories for improvement; it would later turn out to be just the right ones:

- MetroWest resources:

    - Transportation

    - The Serenity Center's peers, food and technology

    - Existence with current housemates

    - Therapy – SVdP, AA, Church, writing

- Normal life musts:

    - Financial foundation and a budget

    - License reinstatement

- Medical Discovery and Discloser:

    - Is there an infection in the new left hip

    - Control of neuropathy in the right leg

    - Discover the reason for the increasing pain from the spine

It was as if something "clicked" or a light switch went on in the brain. I had felt it at the WTC, but that was in a sterile environment with an atmosphere of minimal hope. Now, I was housed with men and women of different ages, issues, backgrounds, education, and motivations. Not in the street, shelter, jail, hospital, or other institution. **This positive change is reflected in what I posted on my Addiction-Reality-Education website:**

- HOPE: Gabapentin is a treatment for alcohol dependence – it is a choice to save your life
http://addictionrealityeducation.com/2016/01/26/hope-gabapentin-is-a-treatment-for-alcohol-dependence-a-choice-to-save-your-life/

- After One Year of Sobriety, Your Brain May Recover
http://addictionrealityeducation.com/2016/05/10/after-one-year-
s...rain-may-recover

- Death: End of the Road for a 27-Year-Old
http://addictionrealityeducation.com/2015/12/12/death-end-of-
the...of-a-27-year-old/

I found myself using the information I had learned in this short time and attempting to relay the results back to others. I threw myself into The Serenity Center and connecting with people I knew from the street. I wanted to help and share what I learned, very subtlety. No one other than my close friends could know about the A-R-E website, my journals, or my future book. I knew that if they did, I would no longer be in their confidence, be a friend, and be able to give back.

Example of a trusted conversation:

Journal 1-16: I just ran into a guy from the old Palladin house. When we talked he told me that he had lived, off and on, under a bridge in Marlborough for three years. He got a job with SMAK repairing houses. He said, "I am living for life."

Reaching for More Foundations of Recovery

MetroWest Resources

The need for transportation: Without a car, the probability of getting even an eight dollar an hour job was low. It was a must that I have transportation around town and to the doctors who were spread throughout the area. Since I was familiar with the MetroWest buses, I could map out the locations I needed to get to and the cost to get there. It was seventy-five cents per ride for people with disabilities. I had no friends and the stigma of living in SMAK Transitional Housing led to many negative responses.

The sad truth is that some people of the subculture would provide transportation only if you provided unreasonable amounts of money or handed over drugs or alcohol. Between the hip infection of the left leg, on and off neuropathy of the right leg, and the spine pain, I needed transportation to doctors in order to attack my disability. Two other very important destinations were the classes I needed to attend to buy my license back from the RMV: two all day classes in Framingham and twenty- four-hour classes in Marlboro.

The subculture's bad side reaches out and touches me: At one of the house floor's weekly meetings, I asked my floor mates for rides and only Leslie said yes. She asked for ten dollars a ride to the classes in Marlboro, which were one mile away and forty dollars to the all-day classes in Framingham, five miles away. Attending was a must because of "the rules" of the RMV. If you miss two weekly classes, you are fined and required to start over. If you miss an *all-day* class, for which you had paid $125, you would lose the money and must pay again and wait for the next available class close to Marlboro. So reliable transportation was critical.

The first sobering event reminding me that I was back in the street culture was the first day of my first ride to a Marlboro class. Fortunately, I had gotten up early to remind Leslie of the ride to class. Leslie, without any hesitation or emotion, let me know that I had to pay seven dollars more than we agreed upon. I looked her in the eyes and said, "I will walk." I walked there and back over a span of 20 weeks, from winter to spring. Walking with my full backpack started to worsen the deteriorated crippled spine and hips.

For the all Framingham classes, I was fortunate enough to reconnect with Paul from the Serenity Center. Paul had to go to these classes at one time and knew my dilemma. So, for $15,

Paul would drive me to Framingham and pick me back up at the end of day. There are good people in the subculture.

The second sobering event involving transportation was the realization of physical disability. While working the bus system, I learned the van drivers are the kings and queens. One dismal day I needed to get to the Center for legal work. While standing on the corner a bus drove by me. It took two phone calls to their headquarters to find out that I was standing on the wrong side of street. Another day I was late, so I had to waddle as fast as I could, cane in hand and pack on my back, but the driver left the corner and he waved goodbye as I got close. There is no describing the feeling of hurt and humiliation. It was not until the day I hit the ice at a bad angle with my cane and fell into an icy street puddle that I broke down emotionally. The people in the cars, waiting at the lights, did nothing to help. I realized my knees and spine would have to fight like hell to get up off the street; *my body was fucked.* It was then that I broke down, shook, and was emotional. It was then that I knew the normalcy of the rehab center and nursing home were illusions. I was not that man with houses, cars, boats, and toys. I was a sober, homeless man, face down on my knee in the ice, water, and mud, wearing brand-new jeans I could not afford.

Journal 1-19: Bad Pain at 3:45 am so I took two Oxys. Went to the S&C and found out that the MetroWest bus 7c, Larry, is a lying piece of shit.

Despite these setbacks, I learned to be where I needed to be at the time I needed to be there. I had the correct change and shut my mouth during the bus rides.

This is just a taste of what I would like you to feel, walking in my shoes as well as those of others you see every day on the street. Those people pushing a cart with bottles or clothes, those people standing on a corner or standing and looking at their feet—they all have a story and not all are bad.

MassHealth PT1 transportation saves the day: The PT1 program of the MassHealth System saves lives. Nicknamed RomneyCare, the health system provides free pickup and delivery for approved medical visits. As an individual, it was my responsibility to learn to use the system.

The startup process was hell, but I learned it. PT1 ended up being a very helpful program. There was no costs and without the transportation to all the doctors, my ability to complete the puzzle of my life changing events would not exist.

The PT1 process starts by a call to your primary doctor's office which then sends a form of approval to MassHealth PT1 department. Once approved at MassHealth, they send a fax to a "contracted transport company." You should always call each organization to see if their part has been done and/or that a form is not just sitting in a fax machine. It was up to me to confirm the ride and the time of pick up each way. If I missed any part of the process, I would go nowhere.

My stay at the Grant Street house was roughly 11 months. 7 months using the **bus***, the* **PT1 forms***, and my* **feet***.*

The Serenity Center Resources – Peer Support

The peers, food, and technology: The Serenity Center is where I learned the most important action items for a person seeking recovery. By watching, interacting, and listening to the people, valuable hypothesis and conclusions could be drawn. At the Serenity Center you can be anyone, wear dirty and grubby clothes, have bad English, and no one will think the worst.

My first two weeks at the Serenity Center were an adjustment period to the people I was reintroduced to and the people who were not there. I immediately met the management. In mellow voices, the same question came at me. Where have you been? You look straight? You back in town?

Journal 1-21: I went to the S&C. I am still an outsider. I need to dress down and check the language; not talk down or in your face mgmt.

Over time the subculture will re-embrace you and let you know what they thought of you before. Over time, others will slowly talk or just say hello. Asking too many questions or digging down into someone's past is not the way or a good thing to do. They will run, shut you down, or you will set them off.

In your face "welcome back":

> One day at the S&C, Len was cooking a normal walk-in breakfast for those who were hungry. Len and I knew the grease and cleaning routine, and I asked if he needed help and what needed to be done. A young adult, roughly twenty-four years of age and ready to fight, interpreted my comments as an insult to Len. Not yet adjusted to the limitations of my body, I gave him a "what is it to you" look. As we moved toward each other I realized both of us were in a no-win situation. I waddled away into the conference room as he was informed by Len to shut his mouth.

A second encounter was with my old friend Benny. Benny had taken to sitting at the computers to play a game whose prizes were points for money. Though illegal at the Center and places like it, no one ever said anything. We had been former drinking buddies at the hotel, the park, and woods, but those days were gone for me and Benny recognized that. Though Benny was using again, and looked it, he still maintained his smarts and the quick use of his tongue. He did not want me there. I was a reminder of his current state and what he might be. Aggression and baiting me for a fight was his plan. To win is not to challenge, otherwise you become part of the problem, so I backed off.

Over time, the twenty-four-year-old man apologized, as did Benny. The young man entered anger management consulting after he cold cocked a man who insinuated that he was gay. Benny became sober, which brought back his gentlemanly personality and smarts, though it only lasted for a short period of time. As time went on, Benny and I would always greet each other with a short, "Hey, how you are doing," not really meaning to know; we liked it, and we remained friends.

Journal: 1-25 I ran into Benny. He just got out of the Marlboro 3rd floor psych. I gave him the Gaba finding on alcohol by Dr. Mason.

I felt the worst for Len. He had helped me when I thought the Burger Hotel was going to be my future. Len had been straight for years, motivated by his desire to see his daughter as she was growing up in the same town. *But he had fallen back. Living in the same places and the same town could have a very high correlation with failure.*

I would later realize that living in the same environment would be a key factor in one's chances to mend the brain. Hanging out with the people in the same place is like waiting for a bus to hit you; maybe it will not happen, but most probably it will. People who came from other towns or environments seemed better able to manage the disease.

Benefits of the Center and places like it: At the Serenity Center I could get regular meals. People who helped around the Center were allowed three picks of quality meats, prepared meals, and desserts to take home. Thanks to the Hannaford Grocery chain, Price Chopper and Panera Bread, the Serenity Center would get weekly deliveries of food that normally would have been thrown in specialized dumpsters due to their expiration dates. I would have top quality steak and other delicious foods, which would typically cost $15 or more at a restaurant. It was during this time of receiving free food and a place to prepare meals that *I started giving thanks at every sitting.* Whether it was just a thought or a five-second meditation, I would remember begging for food, eating chips or raisins, or not eating for days.

Hope-Resources-Will works: As months went by I was in and out of the S&C multiple times weekly. I became more involved with the discussion groups and then started to lead them. During that time, I always wondered if the topics we discussed would help the participants go back to normalcy. I wondered what happened to people I had met along the way. Had any of them turned their situations around? Did all the resources do any good? One day my question was answered:

> It was a normal sunny day when I parked my car in front of the Serenity Center, grabbed my crutches and started towards the door. This time was different. I looked up to see a spotless white Mercedes Benz in front of the door. I immediately reverted to thinking an executive from the corporate office was in the

building and we must all be on our good behavior. Then I went to the front desk and looked down to sign in as always. When I looked up I saw Ruff sitting in as receptionist. Ruff was my friend at the Palladin House and was present when I was threatened by Gary. Ruff was in great shape and looked happy. I asked him, "What are you doing here?" He answered, "giving back." As we spoke I realized it was Ruff's Mercedes Benz. He had left the shelter and worked his way into profitable businesses which moved him out of the streets and into security and normalcy. Not only that, he had just published a book about the streets of Lowell. Since then, we've seen each other on and off. One thing we both agreed upon was the importance of modifying behavior and creating hope and will power. Ruff had made it out of the subculture.

The Grant Street Existence

Men and women of the street culture in one house: Grant Street was not a shelter, but many of its occupants had lived in one. My floor included people of different backgrounds, physical issues, mental problems, substance use disease, and those with a history of using the system. My experiences in the past year and a half were extremely valuable in helping me survive in this house. If I had moved directly from the Palladin Shelter to this sober house a year before, I am not sure I would have been ready.

Without the 90 days to heal, I would not have made it.

I had already run into Leslie who stiffed me for my rides. So, the red flag survival rules returned: keep your head low, do not talk much, listen, never get to close to a person, *and never get involved with the drama.* It seems like common sense and easy to do. But it is not easy when you live with people day after day, night after night, month after month, sharing chores, the bathroom, and the kitchen.

Street language was not hard to adjust to, but it would distinguish those I got close to and those I avoided. We had the hard Boston/New England accents, the Triboro accents, people who used the F word in every conversation, and people who used the F word in every sentence. The requisite good behavior was that everyone to have good hygiene and bathroom manners. The kitchen routine was very similar.

Then there was drama. If I wanted, I could have easily bought what I wanted and brought it to my room. If I had, people on the floor would have slowly suspected, started talking, and maybe even joined me. I was not there for that, considering the low I reached at the Burger Hotel, suffering through the nursing environment, and reestablishing credibility within myself and my supporters. But housemates did it. Ted kept drinking vodka and was taken by police one night after losing it. When you passed by Rick's room, you could always take in that sweet smell. And then there was Guy who had been at the Palladin house with me a year before only to circle back to Grant Street. Guy was still doing the trips to Framingham and shooting up, until the police put an end to that with an afternoon raid of eight police, guns drawn, and covering all the exits. Guy had left the night before.

Recovery is not just the symbolic actions you take and especially not all that comes out of your mouth. A good part of recovery is a deep-down feeling and self-understanding of what you do not want; the fact that you know you will get sick just thinking about it. I have those feelings. Even more important, I now understand the changes and events that happened in my life. By talking with peers and professionals, I could look at the reality of it all.

Tragedy in the first month – June dies: Every so often, I would go to June's office and talk for a short while. She was an interesting character, the type I always liked throughout my life. June was hard talking, street smart, took no shit, with a heart is big as a whale. Occasionally I would ask her why she went out of the way to get me the Mass Housing Grant for a full year. She did not know me, I only had spoken to her on the phone, and had only met her when drove me up to Grant Street. Her response was always the same: "Our conversations said it all. You needed a break."

Journal: 2-9 I went to June's funeral. She was a sweet lady. She went out of her way to get the grant and a room for me. God/angel is on both our shoulders.

June had been a hard Marlboro drinker and smoker. She had stopped drinking, but the smoking was an hourly habit. During my first month at the house, she was scheduled for an exploratory and then a shoulder operation; June had excruciating pain in the shoulder. It was time to attack the problem, she said. June died two days later, on the operating table due to complications with her lungs. She felt no pain.

June's last Masters' miracle was when I asked for a letter stating that I had the grant and was living on Grant Street. The day before the operation, June typed up a letter and placed it under my door. It was on SMAK letterhead, straight to the point where no questions could be asked, signed by June and stating her title.

I knew the importance of documentation and confirmation of a contract. That is why I asked June for the letter. She had come through with flying colors. I had <u>no</u> idea then how important her letter and signature would be to me in the future, nor its importance to my upward path.

The book and the website – tools for normalcy: Truly, the nursing home and June's Grant Street house allowed my brain to repair to the level where I could make decisions and have control over primal urges. My understanding of the "reverse trigger" concept was useful almost every day. Planning my day and my weeks was easy. This led to me gathering all my journals, listing all the places I have been, and contacting the authorities in the organizations that would have my records. I started a crude outline from my notes, which motivated me to write. But I had no laptop except those at the Serenity Center, and writing there would be impossible.

June's miracle happens*:* One day I opened my mail to find a letter granting me fuel assistance. It was unbelievable! I could live in a house for free and not pay the utilities due to government assistance. Tax dollars at work, but in my mind, I had paid hundreds of thousands in taxes over three decades toward that check. I went to the city assistance office to verify the opportunity. They told me I only needed confirmation that I lived in Marlboro and where I lived. I quickly did two things; I registered to vote and received the confirmation documentation. <u>I copied June's letter showing where and why I lived on Grant Street. I sent in the application and forgot all about it.</u> Roughly four weeks later, I received a check in the mail for $785.53 for fuel reimbursement. Some of my subculture peers would have bought clothes, drugs, or used it for rent. I took a bus to the mall and Best Buy. I bought the best 17" laptop I could get for the money, all the latest Microsoft Office software, a protection plan, and anti-spam software. I waited an hour and a half for the bus to come down the road and I stepped on with three large bags that I could hardly carry because of my injured spine. I was now in business. Later that day I made an agreement with my next-door neighbor to pay $20/month for access to the internet. Now the book and the website could become reality; I was working again.

It is very important to make sure you understand that I am not a Bible thumper. But I was in a life that I could never have imagined I would be experiencing. It was a life I did not want my son, my family, or my lifelong friends see me stay in. After leaving the Burger Hotel with Mike and Martin's help and having the operation, events seemed to fall into place. It was as if I listened to a higher source guiding me. I will explain more later but, let's use the website as an example. One comment to Dr. Dwyer, who had written, edited and published books before, led to the completion of the website; was the reason for the website my own therapy, my intention to help people, or both? There are more coincidences, one after another, with far more life changing events to come. Having the technology that before I could not have afforded, and no one would have provided, made a difference.

Real life changing events can happen to anyone. These could be divorce, trauma, a botched operation or financial failure. Each of these can and does lead to masking the pain and hiding the reality of addiction in some shape or form. You, as the reader, just must experience one of these contributors to identify with my circumstances. My life on Grant Street gave me the time to reflect on my past experiences. Yet the most important foundations were to come, enabling me to move forward; they would help me understand what would be necessary for others to have a chance to make it.

Journal: 2-2 Pain is back every day. Oxys were at 6 or 7 when I left the WTC in Westboro. Now I am at 7 or 8.

Therapy in Multiple paths – Keeping Busy

Alcoholics Anonymous: One of the first action items I put on my white board was attending the local AA meetings. I had always carried the big book with me and focused on the 12 steps and accomplishing them; I never had a real sponsor or a person I felt comfortable who would know me. I approach each step by reading and writing. The meetings are always good for listening and learning because of the diversity of addiction that the meetings bring to light. In my mind, it's useful to understand all aspects of the disease.

Then I was introduced to the preaching sponsor who carried the Big Book as if it were the Bible. He was not at every Marlboro meeting with the people he sponsored, yet it only took ten to twenty meetings to educate me on the true purpose of his meetings. He volunteered and was chosen to speak every time. His speaking style was always the same: he started low and ended in a loud dominant voice, never keeping to the topic at hand. I noticed that every time he started to speak, fifteen or even twenty minutes would be used up.

> One particular incident illustrates what I mean. It was a Friday afternoon and the meeting was well-attended. There were always at least one or two new faces and this time there was a new person from Newport, Rhode Island who had just moved into town; she had a cocaine addiction, and she readily shared her story. She finished after five minutes and another local man shared the story of his opiate addiction. Then came the Big Book sponsor with his usual tales of tragedy and successes from the Big Book. Then out of the blue he ended with the comment, "These meetings are for people with alcohol problems! Any other addiction should not be discussed within these walls." The woman from Newport and the other man slowly got up and walked out. They truly believed that the entire group felt that way. Who knows where they went, how they felt, or what happened to them.

I was not a regular visitor after that. I was also fortunate to learn from a Serenity Group meeting that there is a term for what happened: "Recoveryism." Simply put, there are groups and/or individuals who carry only one flag to conquer the disease of addiction. In their minds any other approaches do not work. After that, AA became just a part of the solution picture and I dedicated myself to the "multiple paths" approach to address addictions and/or the disease. See the appendix for more information about Recoveryism.

I wanted to bring this to emphasize the importance of a comprehensive approach to all addictions. Once I regained my license and purchased a car, I was able to attend meetings in the neighboring towns of Northborough and Westboro for diversity sake. Mentioning the event was not intended to slam this individual sponsor; I mention it to caution against inadvertently destroying the chances of others. I never again saw those two people at meetings. The greater good that came from this is the understanding of Recoveryism.

St. Vincent DePaul and the Church: Though two different organizations, both St. Vincent de Paul and the Church both became part of my personal recovery. Having experienced SVdP in Canton, while staying with Mike and Liz, I knew the good they did for those in need. The same priest whom I had met the year before asked the congregation for help starting the SVdP of Marlboro. Sixteen people initially joined, and I was one of them. Within one year, our small group handled over 100 cases and assisted over 60 families. Organizations like this had always attracted me and this had been what I had been looking for a year or so before. I was giving back. I was giving back with the newly-found, hard-won knowledge of the street. I could not have made a better decision and met better people.

Writing and reaching out to friends and family: Armed with a new laptop as well as reports, journals and burning desire to tell my story, I filled part of my days, weeks and months writing. After nine months, Dr. Dwyer and I looked back to acknowledge the five contributors that influenced my descent into addiction. Once I understood the events as they happened, I knew I could now deal with their consequences. It was the best therapy I could have had.

Two of Life's "Musts"

First - financial foundation: It was the beginning of April and I was sitting at my desk overlooking the parking lot. It was Monday morning and I watched the same man pushing his grocery cart, as he did throughout the week. he was picking up bottles and cans for the deposit money they would bring. This morning was a particularly good one because the night before there had been parties going on up and down the street and drug deals in the lots. Even a neighbor gave him the cans piled up in the back of his truck, residue from an after-hours employee party. I wondered how much a can and bottle collector makes in a week.

I had piled my Saturday mail next to the laptop. One of the envelopes had a return address from the Social Security Administration. I opened the envelope to read,

> Social Security Administration
>
> Retirement, Survivors and Disability Insurance
>
> Notice of Award

It did not take more than a split second to remember all the work filling out forms and leaving the nursing home for evaluation appointments. "You are entitled to monthly disability benefits beginning May 15th. You will receive $2,599 on the 3rd of every month. You will also be receiving a lump sum payment for insurance owed starting back to March of last year." It took some time for the shock to wear off, considering I had not had a paycheck of more than $2,000 in over three years. I picked up the phone and told Martin the news. Martin had been the one who kept encouraging me to follow through. He even drove me to the SSDI attorney's office in Quincy. Now it was reality.

Mike, Martin, and I talked about the approval and amount. We concluded that what had helped expedite my approval were the detailed and organized medical records I had presented to the two Federal SSDI doctors who interviewed me.

I was determined to live up to my word to repay the loans friends had given me. I pulled my notes on those loans and sent out checks. Mike thought I was crazy. He encouraged me to keep it all because there would be a time I would need it, but I did what I thought best. Interestingly enough, I later read in the AA Big Book that repaying money is an act of Recovery. I did it because I had sent out emails years before asking for help with a promise of repayment. I had been helped by people like the Goodmans, the Patels, the Foxes, the Garrisons and members of my family; Martin wanted me to wait on him. I paid back a significant amount; it was done.

Journal: 2-10 I have calculated all the SSDI money coming in. I started on the priority payments and the A/R of friends and family.

As the months went by, I could make payments and save cash because I paid no rent. I needed to finish the most important action items before even thinking about stepping out of the culture, if I ever could. Yet, as the months went by, my body was changing and the controlled use of legal drugs to manage pain was working. Staying healthy was my main goal. Being on the street again would be as real a threat to my health as it was when I was in the shelters or walking the streets.

Second - A state license to drive: With the help of Paul from the Serenity Center and the SSDI payment, I was able to schedule, pay, and complete the final class requirements for reinstating my driver's license. Under Massachusetts Law regarding "an Immediate Threat," the rules of a revoked license for the *usual OUI laws do not apply*. Only a meeting with a hearing officer decides your eligibility to get behind a wheel again. *In other words, the hearing officers have your future in their hands*. To prepare for the meeting, I had organized a resume of my positive accomplishments. I also had a reference letter from the Serenity Center about my work, the course completion certificates (and I wore my khaki pants as Martin had always insisted!)

By combining and coordinating the Metro bus and the train, I was able to be in Boston when the RMV opened at 9 am. My stupid mistake behind the wheel, after all the years of driving in control, had changed my ability to achieve some normalcy when I really needed it. Now was my chance to pay the state $500 and get my license back.

When my number was called I stood, holding my cane, waiting for the momentary spine paralysis to fade, while the hearing officer stood and viewed me. What would she think now and would this work against me? We exchanged pleasantries while she reviewed the screen and my history. I reached into my backpack and pulled out the positive file about me, and she started to talk. "Mr. Masters, due to the Immediate Threat, I am requiring you to be admitted to a 90-day closed institution. At the completion of the 90 days, you can come back for the license to be reinstated."

I froze. This person did not know about my voluntary commitment, the shelters, the housing, the fights, the threats, and the shit. All I could see was going into a world of hurt again. But this time, after accomplishing so much, I would not come out better. My spirit would be forever broken. The officer looked up and saw my face. Whether it was the horror in my eyes, my face, or my breakdown shaking and crying, she immediately realized this was a *very bad idea*. "Mr. Masters, wait, there is a way around this. We have a form, which your primary doctor can authorize four times during a one-year period. He or she will be vouching for your driving without alcohol or drugs. I will reinstate your license now under those terms." Still reeling from the thought of 90 days in an institution, I agreed and thanked her. The hearing officer typed her notes into the computer and handed me the form and its instructions. I hurried out into the streets of Boston.

It took four more weeks to arrange a road test and coordinate the time Mike or Martin could drive me, but I got it done. It was a perfect lesson that "driving is not a right, it is a privilege."

*From that point on, I have made it my goal in life to educate others about the terms and conditions of the law regarding **Immediate Threat**. In a nutshell, **there are no rules**. If you are deemed an Immediate Threat, you are at the mercy of the hearing officer. I later befriended a woman who had been a hearing officer for twenty-two years. The bottom line is that the Immediate Threat takes the work off the local or state police. There is no arrest for driving under the* *influence and/or the rules around it. The Registry has the paperwork and control, and if it is not followed, you are without a license, period! No insurance, no transportation for work, and no driving for pleasure. Added to that, the Registry and law enforcement throw the paperwork and responsibility* **squarely on the doctor/medical institution**. *It is a game of pass the buck and you are the loser if one link in the chain breaks. But it is not a game! In my situation, given what I had been through and at my age, this was life or death.*

Total Medical Discovery and Disclosure

It took nine months of dedicated focus and pressure to obtain the doctors' opinions and diagnoses to finally complete the puzzle. My primary doctor, Dr. Ford, was skeptical at first, but as the other doctors' reports and opinions were gathered, he and almost every other surgeon or specialist came to respect my process of analysis and the doctors' summary reports.

Organizing and analyzing it all: It started with my appointment with Dr. Ford. Dr. Ford's last contact with me was just before I hit the streets. I had gone into depression combined with consistent tremors, lower back and spine pain. I masked it with either wine or vodka. Essentially, my credibility was shot and the stigma of alcoholism was in place. Hey, I had to agree and live with it.

Now I was living in the real world and not in a nursing home that required only short walks and an elevator ride. Within the first week of being on Grant Street, the pain in the left groin area would spike to a level 9, especially when I attempted to walk up and down just fifteen steps to and from the second floor. I imagined a small devil with a hot poker and smile on his face. The reality of it all was that I, like anyone else, had to walk to get food, support resources, and make appointments. The pain had to be addressed.

At this point I looked back at myself and asked some questions: what is wrong, when did it start, who is responsible, where should I go, and how do I prove it? The most basic question was, how can I achieve a quality of life given the pain I am in?

The opiate crisis hits home: By now, the death toll due to opiates, pain pills, or heroin in New Hampshire was becoming national news. I kept remembering the doctor down in the City Hospital system. This was the doctor I went to after just leaving Pembrook and when I was living on Darwin Street. Getting pills was not a problem. How was he coping now that the government and medical industry were acting to cover their mistakes and neglect for so many years? Yet, the only relief for my pain was regular and controlled dosages of Oxycodone. This fact runs head on into the stigma in society: *Who believes an alcoholic and at the same time helps him?*

During my first meeting with Dr. Ford, he suggested I consult a pain specialist to validate his opinion. His suggestion led me to create a spreadsheet for reports. If mistakes by the government and the medical profession were going to affect my life, I was going to document everything. It's a page from the playbook of the business, executive, and Human Resource world: "Document everything." So, I did, and it proved to be the best thing I had ever done.

My first document was an extension of what I had started in the WTC for Dr. G. I would log the date, times, level of pain, and number of 5 mg pills I took each day. When I left the WTC, I made sure that I detailed how much I took over and under my allotted number of pills per day. This allowed me to demonstrate control and to correlate the dosage with documented pain resulting from medical mistakes. It didn't take long to convince Dr. Ford of my commitment to control substance use or to convince Mike, my family, and especially Martin.

A pain doctor's validation: I had never been to a pain specialist, so I had no idea what to expect. I decided to provide the doctor with my latest x-rays and MRIs, as well as a summary of the reports I gave the Social Security Disability Insurance doctors.

He had a typical office with a medical assistant and secretary. The walls were covered with certificates and positive articles about his practice. I felt far more comfortable. I sat in the chair next to his desk with the examination table across the room. I started the conversation by letting him know he had all the documentation I had, and asked what he thought could be done. "Mr. Masters, you have two choices. You can have a stimulator implanted in your vertebra, or continue the medication you are on. As it gets progressively worse, adjust the medication." Floored and speechless are the words I would use to express my surprise. I finally responded. "Doctor, I expected you to suggest injections into the spine or the hip. You seemed to skip over that." He responded, "Mr. Masters, in your case, you 'passed Go and went directly to Jail!' We can only manage the problem and the pain. The damage has been done. In all seriousness Mr. Masters, there is nothing pain management medicine can do. You have skipped over any benefit of spinal steroids or therapy."

He gave me the name of the doctor at Beth Israel whom I should see immediately to determine if the stimulator would be an option. The appointment was over. I remember thinking, "At least he was direct and truthful". Now I knew something. His report to Dr. Ford was as follows:

"Impression: Failed back syndrome. Disastrous outcome as above from back surgery at UMass. I think that a spinal cord stimulator may be an option assuming he has no infection at that point."

It is difficult to explain nine months of a rigid schedule of doctors' appointments, tests, and test results. I needed a quick and easy way to let the doctors, especially Dr. Ford, understand examination results. I designed a spreadsheet and divided it by medical practice: Primary, Hip, Spine and Pain Management. At a glance, anyone could follow each critical examination and its final report. Should there be any questions from anyone, I had the reports, x-rays, and MRIs in my brief case. Some of the doctors referred to it as the "red folder." By the sixth and seventh months, the doctors and I were talking the same language and without question, they knew I was aware. Now Doctor Ford and I needed to tackle quality of life. The missing reports were from the hip surgeon and the hospital. I needed to know whether there was an infection in the replacement hip.

Infections just keep coming: Just before leaving WTC, I had been in so much pain that Dr. Siric had ordered an aspiration of the hip to determine whether I had an infection. The results came back positive, but the doctor insisted that it had been from the skin the needle came through. While making a life for myself at Grant Street, it was very common to have my pain flair up around levels 8 and 9. The question was whether it was coming from the hip, spine, neuropathy, or all of the above. Dr. Ford suggested requesting another aspiration from a South Shore hospital. On May 5th, per Dr. Siric's orders, the aspiration was done, and the results were the same. It was at this point Dr. Siric ordered an antibiotic for the pain. The antibiotic would *not eliminate the infection, it would only mask the pain and contain the infection in the blood.* I just wanted to walk again. The aspiration result came eight months and one week after the operation.

Journal: 3-20. Pain is the same. I am only getting five hours of sleep at night. After two hours, the pain wakes me up. I need to move to bed or chair, in different positions. Then I get three more hours.

Again, I had an infection. A medical institution had prolonged a problem, but this time another institution came to my aid. I would recommend that a Consultation Report Spread Sheet (see appendix) should be a requirement of any patient seeing more than one doctor. It took eleven months of pain and hellish days before something was done. Confirmation of the infection eliminated the option of using a stimulator in the vertebrae. I would stay on opiates for as long as it was effective. I am the person for whom those drugs were invented.

The final medical results: After a full year of thorough investigation, opinions, tests and reports, the conclusion was that I am disabled or crippled for the rest of my life. I googled the definition of both words and decided to focus on "crippled." The word is harsh but directly to the point; this was a way of facing my fears and accepting the truth. No more water or snow skiing, no hiking, no tennis, no bowling, no riding watercrafts, and nightly pain flare ups while sleeping; but that does not mean I cannot make life happen in some shape or form. The big question was regarding sleeping with a woman and its pleasure. Was that gone also?

Doctors' Summary Reports:

Hip Doctors: Opinions 1, 2, and 3 concur that there is an infection, except Dr. Siric still is on the fence verbally; he does not recommend a 2-stage replacement.

Spine Doctors: Opinions 1, 2, 3, and 4 concur that there is ARACHNOIDTIS because of the 2011 operation. They will not operate.

Knee Doctor: Dr. Stacey will not operate unless the infection is gone. As of now, the knee is bone on bone due to walking on the streets with heavy weight and years of athletics.

Pain Management: Opinion 1 and 2 concur. The current three medications to mask and control my pain is the only option. Dr. Good's opinion is that my case is highly unusual. He feels that the pain will increase as the back degenerates and the body grows a tolerance to the meds.

Reversal/2 stage replacement: I declined the operation January 20th, one week before the operation. With no friends or partner to live with, I have no rides or support. A nursing home is the only place in which to recover.

In addition to that, Jane and Greg Sellers spoke with a friend who had the 2-stage operation and had major breaks in the "spacer" and other problems. Another story came from the hospital's testing assistant performing my pre-operation aspiration. This person said young men come back for testing for infection even after two years.

Conclusion: I will work with Dr. Ford to control my pain and continue my life as best I can. I will schedule follow up appointments with Dr. Velazquez for antibiotics to mask the infection and Dr. Good about controlling the pain.

Best place to find support: As I concluded my notes and continued requiring my normal needs from Dr. Ford's office, I realized a funny place to find support, a place we may ignore without giving credit where credit is due. That is the nurses, medical staff and office people of my MetroWest's primary. For me, most have heard and/or touched all or parts of my phases in life. Like Lisa, who always greets me with a smile, takes my blood pressure, and very straight forward; and Bani who follows up with me on a Friday night and addresses the very personal details of the case. Brenda, Chris, and Deb who, over time, have seen the pain and the better times. They and others take the time for detail messages to the doctor and/or provide up-beat comments from seeing my improvements. It is important to me because he knew of my addiction and have not judged. They dealt with my physical disabilities and provided positive reinforcement. I know that they know, and still all is good. Their compassion is better than professional therapy and made me stronger.

The Hurt of Stigma – It Should Be in the Plan for Survival

Stigma – do not let it set you back: While recovering physically and mentally, I was gathering resources for positive decisions to come. While still in institutional housing and transitional housing I experienced two negative outcomes from stigma. One was being noticed and coming to grips with being seen as disabled at a business event. The other was when a Talent Manager's attitude and direction did a 180-degree change after viewing my residence via global satellite. Those two events had a very hard sting but nothing that would crush my focus to move forward. I had studied stigma and have been with individuals or groups who were hurt, but I had not yet come face to face with its gut wrenching effect.

Coming out of the abyss: I was now able to move about freely with my legs, spine, and the car I bought with the lump sum SSDI money. This new freedom allowed me to see more family and old friends. I decided to travel within Massachusetts or to New York whenever possible. Many of the people I visited were those who witnessed my struggle with the disease and provided me with money and shelter until I came back. Well, I had reached that point, and I was back. I had made my amends, thanked everyone, repaid debts, and gone back to my real personality.

Now I could step out on my own, reinforced by the knowledge I had done the best I could. I visited people and was invited to visit. During these visits, I observed a high correlation between the dinner table conversations and verbal reinforcement of the negative; a feeling of superiority. I noticed that during dinner conversations that some people readily accepted me despite my struggles, while others could not get over the stigma associated with the disease.

This conclusion came from comments made to me about my own circumstances and those who have confided in me about their experiences. My interactions allowed me to easily size up the person's true attitude.

This all happened during my first "stepping out" into the normal world. Two events set me back on my heels, but as I thought about the comments and emails, I felt stronger despite these individuals' ignorant assumptions.

During one of my car trips, I was confronted with two similar comments and assumptions within 24 hours. One time I was leaving a house, so I could meet an old girlfriend at a restaurant with a bar. As I was leaving, a relative expressed a serious concern for where I was going; "It is not a good idea to meet at the bar. It goes against the rules of recovery and you could relapse." The other instance was calling a friend and letting him know I arrived in town and to meet me at Hauller's, a restaurant we had frequented throughout our lives. His serious voice demanded, "What are you doing there? I hope you are not having a drink."

Both comments hurt because they betrayed a lack of confidence or a stereotype about an AA member. These people care for me and wanted me out of harm's way. Unfortunately, people need to learn that beating addiction is a practice of multiple approaches. Organizations like AA and SMART are only one or two lanes on the highway.

Meeting the Foxes at their lake house was complicated. A typical outing at their place involved water sports, food and drinking. I could have lived with two out of three, but fun was not on the agenda, and the first day's activities and comments set the stage for disaster. Later that night I remembered that the traditional evening consisted of cards and drinking, neither of which my system or my wallet could take. One of the Fox kids asked me, "Why are you here?" The shots were poured, and my friend was laughing at me. I realized that going any further would undo all the work done by people who cared for me. So,

I stood up, poured the shot they had poured for me down the drain, and walked to the living room to sleep. One of the last statements I heard that night was, "I told you not to invite him!" Sober and straight I remained.

Business stigma is a category unto itself. What was not there before is now seen clearly by others in the professions where I made a living

The stigma became real life at a job fair in Westborough on a March afternoon. Even with 10 mg of Oxy and an Aleve, my ability to hold my walk was futile. I ran into an old friend who noticed me walking with tiny steps and asked about the problem. I summarized what happened and the result. I commented that it crippled the legs and I must live with it. It was then he said, "Brian, you are disabled, not crippled!" I just stared at him. His looked away, realizing what he said. It made no difference. They cannot call it Social Security Crippled Insurance, it must be "Disabled" to be accepted. I wondered if my disdain for my situation would ever wear off, but I knew the professional stigma may always remain.

Stigma – There always will be stigma. Coming to terms with stigma is a must. Events that happened in the past will continue to be brought up in conversation because people will always associate the person with the negative addictive behavior of the past, even if it no longer exists. I experience severe hurt when a friend, relative, or business acquaintance brings up the past or, even worse, reacts as a mother would, as if to say, "This is better for you because I know the way you will react." The only choice is to live with it and move on.

Separation for Recovery's Sake – or Not

Choices – Pay the Money and Stay or Move Out

*As the one-year grant was coming to an end, I had to decide whether to pay the monthly rent for the SMAK room on Grant Street or use Craigslist and find a place of my own. **This would be a room outside a regulated environment**. The cost of living at the SMAK house was $85 per week or $340 per month. This is a price that cannot be matched anywhere, even in subsidized housing. I had to weigh the cost against my plan to get back to normalcy in some shape or form. I wanted a real life like I had before, building businesses, an estate, and a family. Due to hard work and good fortune I was on my feet again. It was decision-making time.*

Day after day, week after week, month after month: I had gotten to know the people on my floor very well. After eleven months, I had a routine that worked for me to get things done and avoid conflict. But was it where I wanted to be? Volunteering for St. Vincent DePaul of Marlboro and working at the Serenity Center were rewarding and gave me something to look forward.

The fact remained that the people would change, but the culture would stay the same. There would always be individuals I could easily communicate with like John and Steve, and others I could not relate to at all. Yet, the reality of the culture would still be there every time I put the key in the front door.

Two events sealing my decision to move:

A regulated house stigma: For me, there was never even a chance of having guests. There were no overnight quests. No sleep over by anyone; no true home environment. Then there was the event that sealed my decision.

A man named Larry came over to deliver food from the food pantry. Over time we became friends. As I was talking in the hall with my door open, a temporary manager from SMAK came down the hall speaking in a very loud voice. "I am the filling in for Betty, so if anyone has any issues, I will be down stairs." Larry looked at me very puzzled. I told her, "Can't you see that I have a guest?" Her response was, "That is okay, honey, you are allowed guests between 8 and 7." Humiliation was not the word, and I could not describe the look on Larry's face. He only said, "I did not know this was a form of jail, I will not ask why."

Job Loss- Human Resources uses the internet: During the holidays I altered my goal to see if I could get a job back in Syracuse or the Skaneateles area. Once again, my current living situation slapped me in the face.

During a phone interview with a Talent Manager from Welch Medical Devices, in Skaneateles NY, the man asked, "Brian, do you own your own home"? I said, "No, I have an apartment in a rental complex, so I can easily move back to Syracuse. Why"? "I am looking on Zoom at the address on your resume. I was not sure if you rented the house out or rented a floor. I can see the signs on the front of your building!"

Five years before I had warned my friends who faked addresses or had two jobs at once that social media such as LinkedIn or Zoom would catch up with them. I was right, but this time social media kicked me in the ass. The Grant Street address, when viewed from a satellite, showed the house, the signs on the walls, the cars, the street people, and the culture surrounding it. Chances for a high paying job ended with the manager's computer and so did the interview.

Grant Street was transitional housing and it was time for me to transition out.

Time to measure successes for my next decisions: It had been a long eleven months with many life experiences. I had to look at where I had been, where I was now, and where I wanted to be. I had made plans along the way, but most did not materialize. However, when I reviewed the goals and the results, I was encouraged:

- MetroWest resources:

    - Transportation - **Done**

    - The Serenity Center, food and clothes - **Done**

    - Existence with current house mates – **Done**

    - Therapy – SVdP, AA, Church, writing – **On going**

- Normal life musts:

    - License reinstatement - **Done**

    - Financial foundation and follow a budget - **Done**

    - My looks - eyes, face, and hair – **Work in progress**

    - Moving out of Transitional Housing – forever – **Work in progress**

- Medical Discovery and Recovery:

    - Is there an infection in the new left hip – **Done, confirmed**

- Control of Neuropathy in the right leg – **Done**

- Discover the increasing pain from the spine - **Done**

I had established a beachhead from which to move out to normalcy. When Virginia Dwyer and I started to discuss what transpired in the last year of so, whether by planning or by luck, it all came together; 90 days of abstinence, being away from people or an environment that could have a negative influence, correct medical help for pain, transportation, good family and peer support and more.

The foundation had been set. Later, I will piece together the "life critical musts" I had achieved and how it mirrors what the recovery and stigma experts currently teach. This is what should happen to save your life.

For some, the key foundation block for recovery is the rule to move and/or separate from the people and environment that could cause relapse. This key fact applies to all addictions. For example, a gambler should not go to the local bar where bets a being placed. For example, Russ, my friend at the Paladin, did not improve his path by staying where he was comfortable.

The First House for Normalcy – Failure

The decision: Within one week of putting my request on Craigslist, I received a call from Jonathan who had a room in his house on Sears Street in Marlboro. He mentioned that the cost was $500 per month and included use of the kitchen and laundry room. The rent would come with internet and 120 cable channels on a 45" HD TV. On my second visit, I paid the first months' rent and security deposit. I was *really* moving.

Of course, I scheduled the move with Mike and Martin, my trusty legs and lifting buddies. I dreamed of the old days we would have had cocktails moving out and cocktails moving in; then I would have paid for a dinner at Capital Grill at forty dollars a plate. The "reverse trigger" wiped that thought out of my mind. We had fun anyway.

An environment that I wanted: All that Jonathan had promised and put in the lease was accurate. I had use of the kitchen, living room, and the bathroom. The neighborhood was what I wanted and needed for the next steps in my plan. The street was safe, the area was good, and best of all it was quiet; there were only sporadic ambulance and police sirens, night and day.

Martin had made it his mission to put a lock on my vintage 1890 room door. It took days of measuring, trips to the hardware store, and placing screws, but that lock was solid and provided a secure place to come and go.

I quickly let friends and family know I had moved, as well as St. Vincent DePaul and the Serenity Center. People could pick me up or come in and talk; there were no rules of the street culture hanging over my head. I thought I was moving up.

In November 28th and out February 2nd: It was not apparent with just three visits that I was not the only person living in the house. Jonathan had seven people living in a two-story, 100-year-old house and every one of them was living the life of the subculture I was attempting to escape.

The two-bedroom apartment upstairs was rented to a husband and wife in their twenties with two children. The children were in grade school, he was trying to get SSDI, and I do not know what she did. I do know they owed $4000 in back rent, partied, and had the known pusher visit every weekend. Living in the cellar was a young man in his twenties and his occasional girlfriend. He could come upstairs to use the bathroom and shower. The lock Martin had meticulously worked on became worth its weight in gold.

As we walk through these events and watch the people I encounter, it starts to become apparent that there are methods and actions to beat the disease and step into a normal world. Being exposed to the same people with whom you had partied and being around similar individuals with destructive lifestyles can destroy you. You must to get away from it. This was a street culture that still had its trademark. Everything else was essentially the same.

The last straw was when Jonathan allowed Steven to come live on our floor and sleep on the chair in the living room. Jonathan recruited people from the Serenity Center to work odd jobs at the four houses he owned. In return for work, Steven could be off the street, sleep at the house and be fed: slave labor or indentured servant were the terms I used. For the sixty-two days I lived at that house, Steven was there for forty-one. Then came the usual behavior from these tenants: a dirty kitchen, the smell of sweat and urine from dirty clothes, liquor bottles in the trash and yard, missing food, noise.

I put my ad back on Craigslist, hoping not to make the same mistake again.

Craigslist:

> Posting body: I am a sales professional looking to rent a one bedroom with access to a bathroom.
>
> My background: I lived in Westborough for 21 years, raising my son. He is now in Hollywood, CA, so the rental is only for me. I belong to the Civic Club, SVdP of Marlboro and other organizations. I have been in the high-tech software industry for 32 years and will continue to sell.
>
> I need access to the internet, cable TV, and off-street parking.

Salvation comes from a text message:

Within two days of reposting the ad I received a text asking if I had found an apartment. She had a house in Westborough with a room available. I responded by asking the price and if she had pictures. She sent them the following day. My 2002 Subaru Forrester could not get me there fast enough.

I'm Finally Home

Life Rebuilds Itself – I can make a new ending

Too good to be true: While driving over to Westborough I reviewed my budget and whether I could afford the increase in rent. The pictures of the place were fantastic, but I needed to reel in my thoughts for potential disappointment. Finding the street was easy with my GPS. I was wearing my khakis, blue polo shirt, sweater, and $100 sneakers. I was good to go.

I pulled into the driveway and a fully restored antique farm house stared me in the face. As I got closer, I could see the property included the house, a modern barn with horses, corrals, a four-car garage and parking spaces close to the barn.

The landlord waved as she was entered the barn, leading a black and white spotted horse at least five and half hands high. After Sheryl put the horse in the stall, she walked briskly to me with hand extended. "Glad to see you, let me show you the place and you can tell me what you think."

The house: My tour of the house started in the living room, appointed with a 50" HDTV, couches and chair, eight-foot pool table, a beautiful hardwood floor, and a low wood beamed ceiling. We then entered the kitchen, which had two refrigerators, center island, pull-out shelving, compactor, and dishwasher. The kitchen was connected to the porch, which was adjacent to the in-ground pool. The entire downstairs had polished hardwood floors. The living room could have fit six of my rooms on Grant Street, twenty of my bed areas in the WTC nursing home, and was twice the size of the men's bunk room at the Palladin shelter.

The bedroom was like the downstairs and in perfect condition. It had a brick fireplace and walk-in closet. The pool table, cable, internet, three bathrooms, outside pool, and use of the twenty-four acres were all included in the monthly rent of $750, the maximum I could afford. Any other comparable living space in the area would cost twice as much.

We sat in the kitchen and discussed the details. There were no rules, just common sense and courtesy. "We are all adults," Sheryl said. There was no lease and the payment was on the first of the month. As she was asking, "Do you like it," I was pulling out my wallet and a check. Sheryl mentioned that there was one thing I should be aware of and that was, "My two small dogs can wander the house and the land outside but within their perimeter. Is that okay?" The deal was done.

The address was 1 High Street and that is how I felt, "high." From here I could work on the job search, do my volunteer work, write, and start a more normal existence. There would be no "F word" as an adjective, police with guns drawn cuffing men, or property being stolen. It was up to me to keep focused and not to lose perspective. I had learned and experienced a lot in my former life. Even more in a life of literal survival. The challenge would be to balance what I had learned in order to live in both worlds, simultaneously, for now.

Journal: I spoke with Johnny and it was a great conversation. He is learning how to get to the next step in his industry. I pray all the time that my Angel will be on his shoulders.

The move: Mike and Martin were there for me again but this time we knew it was different. My personal items fit like a glove in the Westborough room. I placed the six-draw antique wooden desk near a window, so I could look over a road frequented by joggers, not men with shopping carts or doing drug deals. Mike returned my oriental rug, which I had given to him as collateral two years before. It complemented the polished wood floor perfectly. I placed the double bed was against the wall and adjacent to the window overlooking the stables.

Enjoying the sounds of life: I opened the windows as the weather got better. In the morning, while I took my meds to reduce the pain, I listen to birds chirping to each other at sunrise. The added benefit was the occasional whinny of a horse in the barn. Everyone in the house had his or her own routines and lives. If no one was at home and I was alone, I would stand in the middle of the living room or kitchen and raise my arms just to feel that vast amount of space around me, shared by no one at the time. For the last two and a half years, I had been in rooms shared by no less than four people at any time or a bedroom only five paces long or wide. Now I did not lock my door, and I did not expect problems from other people. In other words, no drama.

Reestablish the good from the past: An event in Westborough created a comfort zone for me moving back and subduing the drama from my past.

> Within one week of being back I was asked to attend a Civic Club meeting, which was now held at a bar that I had frequented many times in the past: The Place Hotel. For over a decade I had gone there with or without family to have drinks and rub elbows with coaches and townies. During my divorce I had introduced Jennifer Peroni to The Place, and she ended up being absorbed into their friendships and relationships. In other words, a lot of drama. It also was a known hotel for men down on their luck. The first month I had become homeless I had begged the manager of the hotel for a room at $100 per week; unfortunately, they were renovating and taking no boarders. Now, two years later, I walked through the door and saw many familiar faces doing the same old

thing. Of course, there was Steve the manager, from whom I had begged for a room, working the bar. Before I went into the meeting, Steve made a point of saying he was happy for me. I told him, "I was dead broke and on the street, all the times I had called." His response was, "That is why I am happy for you. You look great and on your feet." It was the last thing I thought would make me feel fantastic, a comment from a man I thought couldn't have cared less.

I was back: I was back as much as I could be under the circumstances. I had learned about the contributors and effects of the disease, and how they paved the road to my demise. I felt nothing could hold me back except my health, and that was work in progress every day. Now I could have visits from friends and family, even Johnny and his girlfriend. Yes, Johnny. Johnny was a loose end, so now I included him and his lifestyle in a new set of plans.

I was extremely committed to providing help and continuing self-discovery at St. Vincent de Paul and at the Serenity Center. I felt it was time to use what I had experienced to help others on a path to a happier life. Still, it was important that these two worlds remain separate. Neither, in my opinion, would understand the other. I would end up being shunned by both.

Because my license had been reinstated, I could drive anywhere. I used my reserve money to go and see Johnny. I didn't know what he thought of me, nor did he have a clue about all I had been through. Whether it turned out bad or good, a father is obligated to make a try; it is the son's obligation to better understand his father.

Set Straight a Bad Contributor - A Trip to Los Angeles:

I cannot hide from myself-disabled: It was a new experience when I hit Logan Airport. I literally could not walk to the counter without a break due to the pain; I made sure I took two 5mg tabs of Oxy so I could walk and sit without grimacing in pain. I had been in airports most of my life and never before needed assistance walking the terminals at O'Hare, Atlanta, Denver, and Heathrow in England. My personal reality had changed, and I had to adapt. Jet Blue brought the wheelchair and I was officially labeled "disabled" for the entire flight and the connecting flight. We blew through check-in, security, and went directly to the gate.

I felt most vulnerable when the airport staff left me. The pain limited my ability to get to a bar and bathroom only thirty yards away. The reality was, *this is what I was now*, yet it was impossible to bury my memories of business trips and family vacation flights. These thoughts led to a new conclusion: what company would hire an older man with limited mobility to meet a client or a company consultant at the airport? Who would take the chance or assume the liability?

This trip taught me who I was physically. And that was that.

It was worth every penny: From the time Johnny and I met to the time I left, we worked on a new understanding. He was now a grown man looking for that next career step and had developed a life of his own. It was my job to listen, observe, and connect with his way of thinking.

The fact that I needed urine bottles by the bed because I could not get to the bathroom in time did not matter. The fact of seeing my right leg brace so the knee would not grind bone on bone did not matter. It was a long overdue reunion right down to watching the Patriots win a playoff game.

There was no need to rehash the missed phone calls or off the wall comments. Talking about it or expressing our feelings would do no good now. But one thing came across. I was myself again and he knew it. By the last day, his respect for me came back. I could even give him advice and he listened.

> The day before I left, Johnny received a call for a position at the largest communication/television network in the world. That phone call led to hours of discussions between us about job roles, verbal control, and business techniques. We planned together again. The interview led to his working on a pilot as the next step in his creative business world.

Johnny and I parted at the LAX airport as father and son--a father and son with a new understanding of where each person was coming from. Johnny did make one comment which connected my past behavior to the present. He said, "It is obvious that you have come a long way." That was my beachhead with Johnny. Within the month he would call me, not just to say hello but also to get advice on finances, his jobs, and friends' attitudes. This is what I had been looking forward to since he had been born. I think any father hopes for those moments. We had that relationship until the divorce. Now, maybe, we could pass Jail and go directly to Go.

It became obvious from the first week of the move back to Westborough that events, people, and my health would test my resolve. The hardest part was to continue helping people through the acts of kindness of St. Vincent DePaul of Marlboro and being a supporting member at the Serenity Center. Between the A-R-E website, volunteering, and the book, I hoped that I could help people who wanted to help themselves.

I had no answer within me or from trusted friends whether to cut the rope and leave the last three years behind or achieve a balance between then and now. I know for a fact that the corporate world, either high tech or retail, would NOT want to hear it. So, I put my faith in The Path, which seemed to work events for the better.

A Cell Call Brings Respect and Work Opportunity

I was now back to having a clear head and being the competitive and the talented sales person I was prior to 2010. Mike and I were communicating almost every day by text and getting together once a month. Our conversation topics had changed from my environment and my daily issues to Mike's bosses and working the sales job he had been desperately trying to hold on to. The difficulty of keeping a high paying and high-profile software and services sales job at our age was a common topic. I had the benefit of listening about the deals and occasionally sitting in on conference calls with the internal management or a prospect. I was chomping at the bit to get back into the high-tech sales. After decades of success, I had a feel for business and when the timing was right. Mike and I were talking strategy and tactics with mutual respect and no condescension. It was a huge step forward.

The phone call: One afternoon as I was driving back from Mike's house I received a call from Larry Thompson, an old networking business partner and end-user consultant. He said, "Brian, I just completed my seven-year contract in New Jersey and took a job with a retail services company out of Manchester, New Hampshire. I want to catch up."

It was midway through the conversation that I let Larry know of my three-year departure from the industry and the fact that I was disabled. I felt he or anyone else we knew did not need to be informed of hospitals and shelters. Larry suggested a 1099 contract. This would mean working for the company as if I were a contractor. I would not be paid until a deal was brought to the table. Larry commented, "Brian, this would allow you the ability to get into the swing of things and make money in the process." His offer was so timely and unexpected that I missed the exit to 495 North and kept going toward Providence, RI.

I agreed.

Journal: Randy D. and Mike H. want me to work for them. I am very proud. Very few come back.

A Full Time Sales Job for a Disabled Man

A resume sent: It was a fact that I was back to the clear headed, competitive, and talented sales person I was prior to 2010. I knew it! At this point I felt it was an issue of accepting a job that allowed me to use the Oxys to control obvious pain. As part of my weekly schedule, I would learn the new social media job-seeking strategies and send out selective resumes. Four months after I moved into Westborough, companies started reaching back to me.

In the beginning of June, I received a call from EMS to sell Internet and Cloud based payment services. EMS was investing in a committed growth in telemarketing and direct sales; in other words, start expanding for sales and revenue. This time I decided to pursue the full hiring process and see where it led. One Wednesday I drove to Framingham to meet the EMS Regional Sales manager, Tom Larkin. Much to my surprise, Tom's management style was much like mine when I successfully opened Sun Data's offices in the Northeast, ultimately leading to my millionaire status. Tom had two individuals making six figures, and he needed four more to complete his objective. The marketing and sales plan was sound, pay and overrides were achievable, and my prospecting plan would work. I decided to accept.

To get off on the right foot with Tom, his boss, and others in the office, I also decided to explore stabilizing my disability. I was in pain, but wondered if I could stabilize and isolate the problem. I let Tom know that further testing was needed. I felt good after our conversation since Tom commented that the position was available to me; he knew I would lead in expanding the Region. The start date was left open.

Recovery Needs Good Health

My Health Puts Any Jobs on Hold

Pain raises its ugly head: The critical factors were the complications in my hips, back, and legs. I would manage the pain in one area only to have another area go between Level 8 or 10 on the pain schedule. I was counting the Oxys every day by me and I controlled its usage. As time went on, the infection in the left hip required less pain meds, only to have the right hip be ground down to bone on bone, crushing together. Now the pain in the right hip happened every time I stood, walked, or sat down. The "resection" operation was the option recommended by a majority of the surgeons to rid the body of the infection, so the right hip could be replaced at a future date. The other option to eliminate the pain and walk again was a standard replacement of the right hip, despite most surgeon's refusal to do so because of potential complications and liability.

Pain control remained the same until five months after the move to High Street. Now the right hip, right glute, and thigh were in pain while standing or walking. This was something new. It wasn't just neuropathy from the 2011 operation, but chronic pain in the right hip area.

The pain had gotten so bad that I had to limit my driving to a minimum. The pain of swinging the legs in and out of the car was terrible, depending on the day. I avoided taking extra visits to the bathroom or kitchen, which means, I was sleeping, watching tv, or on the internet and writing. Using ice, Litho pads, and Oxycodone gave me some relief.

Sleeping: Sleeping or laying on my back for long period of time was difficult. First the pain touched the small of the back, and then it joined by the hip pain. The best position, up to that point, had been laying on my left side. Now, the pain did not stop when I repositioned. Techniques like a pillow between the legs and an ice pack were fruitless.

From then on, I would get out of bed, take an Oxy, wait until it took effect, and then sleep in my desk chair with the pillow on my laptop. I experimented with every over the counter pain reliever and even borrowed a muscle relaxer; nothing worked. The side effect from this position was the agony of moving and standing when I woke up, plus swelling in the right foot.

As I reflect back, I do not remember how it is to have a day without pain.

Back to a Boston hospital: I pride myself on the work and opinions done the previous year to find out the consequences of the problem operations and diagnosis miscalls. Dr. Ford, my Westborough chiropractor friend, nicknamed SiS, and I decided it was time for a second opinion on the new problem by the best Boston Hospital, New England Baptist.

Doctor King agreed to bring me in for a consultation.

After I registered I was referred to the x-ray department for the x-ray Doctor King had ordered. My wheelchair arrived, and I was transported to the left wing and seen immediately. After the x-ray, I was transported down one floor to Dr. King's office and brought to one of the three waiting rooms.

Dr. King showed me the x-rays. The x-rays taken that day were placed next to the x-rays taking by Shields just eight months prior. Dr. King pointed to the small white spot on the joint from eight months ago. He then pointed to the non-existent ball and joint on the x-ray taken an hour before. The connection to the ball and joint was indistinguishable and the haze around the area complicated the view.

Diagnosis: "Significant amount of advancement of his osteoarthritis. He has femoral head collapse and severe joint space destruction." Simply put, I was and would continue to be a wreck below the waist, and the hip needed to be replaced.

The complication was that the infection in the left hip still existed and was masked only by an antibiotic I had been taking. No institution or doctor would replace either hip or the right knee without eliminating the infection first.

One night in July I knew the pain had come to a tipping point. I took my muscle relaxer and one Oxy an hour before turning off the TV and lifting my legs into the bed. Once in bed, my right hip and the small of my back went into shock mode at a pain level 9.5 and 10. I could not stop my body from thrashing about until I flung myself into my desk chair.

I could not get to the other side of the room, let alone empty my piss jugs into the bathroom. I could put no weight on the right side at all. By morning and four additional Oxys and 650mg of Anacin, I reached out to Mike and Martin for crutches. At the same time, I called Dr. Ford and Dr. King to see what hospital I should go to if I needed an ambulance.

I had reached my beachhead of normalcy, just waiting for next step forward toward happiness and purpose. Then came the fact that my health was not going to cooperate.

Can it be eliminated? We were sure on one point. The only way to eliminate the infection was a two-stage resection of the left hip which involved a seven-month process of flushing my system with antibiotics, testing, taking me off the antibiotics, testing, then more antibiotics. If the infection was cleared, a new left prosthetic hip would be implanted; then I could proceed with the right hip at a future date. If the infection was not cleared, I would be without a left hip forever; the right hip and right knee would always be in pain.

A Second Surgery Option

Provides New Hope

Another one of Martin's ideas

Martin's comment strikes pay dirt: Martin and I sat at a Panera in Westboro and pondered the reality of my getting back as much as I had, only to be subjected to pain and/or a lengthy operation. Martin tapped me on the arm and said, "Go see Dr. Siric! He has not been approached and he knows your history." It took a day to sink in, only because it was the same South Shore Hospital where I contracted the infection in the first place. Yet, I had everything to gain and Boston City would still be available.

Doctor Siric's decision: I met with Doctor Siric twice. The first time he reviewed newly taken x-rays and made the statement, "Brian, you cannot live like this! Even with a slight infection in the left, the right needs to be replaced. Based on new aspiration findings, I will do the operation, so you can walk. With that understanding, we are walking into this with eyes wide open."

The aspiration was done after two weeks of purposely withholding the antibiotic. It was the second appointment and Dr. Siric reaffirmed his decision to put in a new right hip. All that was needed was my signature on the forms and to schedule a date.

Now there a second option and time for a decision: It was now my call on whether to do the revision or go directly and replace the right hip. It was estimated that the pain reduction would be from 9 to 1 or even 0. But what of complications?

With the beachhead of addiction recovery firmly in place, now I had the decision to correct health issues that had contributed to my addiction path. It was time to make my choice to move ahead to normalcy once and for all.

Every day: Every day I would think of my journey and the lessons learned. The goals had been met, except for obtaining a job for financial stability and self-respect. That would have to be put on hold until my healthcare action plan had been accomplished. This book may not end with me walking into an office building, briefcase in hand; that may happen at another time. This ending is reality for me. The lessons learned are for you.

Time for "Reflection"

Journal: 1-22 – I am still crying, and I have no control, but it is good. I know that 2011 led to a break in reality. So, I have a feeling of a waste of 3 to 5 years. They are years I cannot retrieve.

Recovery was not over night: At this point I felt great. I not only had a clear head, but I had a deep feeling inside that things and people around me were good. It was time to reflect back and for my own satisfaction, understand what I had done right to turn this around.

In retrospect, my ability to work towards normalcy was from September of 2015 to February of 2017 and continues to this day. My stays in an institution allowed me the time to understand the contributors that brought me to addiction and robbed me of hope. The street and time had broken the body, so a surgeon stepped in to help. Now, there was time to repair the most important part of the body, the brain, to be able to reason and think for myself. What followed is a series of events which set a firm foundation built by blood, sweat, and tears. I was ready for working paths toward recovery and a new and happy life.

Among the best sports philosophy by a coach I had heard were the comments by Bill Belichick of the New England Patriots before and after winning his fifth super bowl; it was about his players who were hurt. The press and public were asking why some of the injured players were not on the field since they were medically sound. Bill's comments focused on rest and sleep. Not getting back on the field and knocking heads but repairing the body and the mind by sleep are essential components of success.

I stuck to what I had learned from the classes and on the street. I had started with the brain and gave it time to heal. A 90-day recuperation is what any person with addictive behavior needs for a solid chance to recover. The health system and its process of putting an individual on the 3rd or 2nd floor of a hospital only to release him after four days does not work.

> During one of my conference calls with Dr. Dwyer, she asked a very good pointed question. "Brian, if you had not had to go into the Westborough Transitional Facility for over 90 days, time for your brain to repair, would you have recovered as well as you have? That question floored me at the time even though I knew the answer a year before. "NO," I responded, "my brain would not have been ready."

Next was separation! The time away took the people, shelters, houses, and the street out of the equation. I asked for the time to stay at the WTC when there was nowhere else to go. By staying away from the people and places that had become a comfort zone, the chances of false hope, complacency, and the desire to mask the pain were gone.

Then there was support: Support from friends in the area who extended the time and energy to do the necessary next steps. For me, it was working on a relatively safe place to live and gathering the reports relating to the trauma I had been through. Complementing the face to face support were the texts, voice mails, and conversation which became normal.

Financial: It was extremely important to achieve a baseline financial objective. I was alone and single and receiving $2,500 per month. If I had never qualified for SSDI, I would have needed income that would put me in a comfortable position in order to make the big jump back to the software industry. With good health, I would target a position at $16 per hour for 40 hours per week, for a total of $2,560 a month. Many people combine multiple jobs to achieve their financial goals. It depends on your motivation and ability, but a baseline income can be achieved and is important for everyone.

Organizations and planning: Being in the "real world," I used any support and resources I had available to me to supply my needs. I worked and depended on friends to help me out and provide positive motivation. I used churches, the Serenity Center, MassHealth, and other organizations to provide basics such as food, therapy, and housing. The time on Grant Street provided transportation, self-motivation, planning, and additional support as it came along.

Loved one: Family plays an important role. A new and improved relationship with family is one of my most significant rewards. To me, family is everything; it is the core of a person as far as I am concerned. Johnny's relationship, as well as interaction with the Sellers, Beth and Jack, Mike and Liz and James and Clare are most important; we care about each other.

Medicine: Using all the assets and opinions I could, we finally found a balance through meds. Medicine for the pain and medicine for the addiction.

I am so convinced that these fundamentals are the keys to success, I listed them in the A-R-E website as the 11 Action Plans to create the beachhead to normalcy. One week when I was working at the Serenity Center, I was asked to lead a discussion on William White's Recovery Capital Statement* and what it means for those in recovery. I studied its suggested use of assets and a path to recovery. It struck me hard when I realized that the thirty-five statements Bill White uses for individuals to better themselves parallel my path. For some reason I felt assured, that I, with a lot of help, used the assets with positive results.

S. Paul was the officer of the court, who recognized my dilemma as a result of the individuals and the Burger Hotel. As an officer to the court and resident, he witnesses subculture situations and life style continuously. I later met with S. Paul and discussed potential solutions/help for long term addicts. His comments, which I agree with, were such that I had to share them with you:

> "In my estimation, that lifelong recovery is a commitment that lasts a lot longer than "90 days". It needs to be a continuum that first focuses on detox and then be committed to distance the individual from their past life and put them on a life that is remote from their source of addiction. Segueing to living in a group setting, to a supervised living situation where they exist in a standalone setting, then leading to incorporating into a new community away from their past with the hopes of a future that is productive and rewarding for themselves and much distant from their old source of addiction."

> However, this will never happen without a sincere commitment from the medical community and funding by the Governor and/or the federal government.

Journal 8-17: William White, top author on recovery and stigma, likes my work and would like to read the book when it is done. He volunteered to be a pre-publishing trial reader. But he and

Dinsmore cannot help with a publisher. Publishers are getting a bad name.

What a Ride – Success or Not

Remember: Remember the initial contributors to my addiction and the belief that there was no hope. Remember my attacking the problem multiple times, only to fall into a subculture/street culture world as the health system failed. Remember all those meetings, shelters, houses, people, staff, nurses, police, tears, and smells. Then remember it is possible to rise from the ashes by lucky circumstances, planning, actions, and hope into a world, in which you can choose to continue to live.

In my case, the last choice for a healthy, pain free living had to be made. Once completed and if successful, I could look forward to employment and renewed self-respect, with the help of the multiple paths. The choices were clear. One, I could undergo a reversal to clear the infection, even if it takes months, in order to have surgery on the painful right hip. Or else I could opt for immediate surgery on the right hip, potentially eliminating the debilitating pain, but risking the spread of the infection.

Questions: Was my path successful? As the key elements for a normal quality of life were put in place, did I get where I wanted to be? NOW, if you were walking in my shoes, was this ride successful? I know what I think and feel, but this book is not just about me. Would the 11 Action Plans for a Beachhead (see Appendix) work for others suffering from addiction? Would Dr. William White's Recovery Capital Scale and planning work? You have seen what I did to move out of the street culture/subculture and achieve the opportunity for a "new ending." It is up to you to decide and act.

Understand that the decision for surgery could only be made with the clear head of recovery. Without the cognitive ability of a healthy brain, another disaster would be waiting to happen. Due to the multiple lanes of the recovery highway, the disease was in remission. Now there were choices that any normal person would have to make.

Observations Not to be Overlooked

Facts to Think Through

Life's events set a stage: I was fortunate or unfortunate, depending on how you look at it, to have encountered so many contributors to addiction. Unfortunate because of the obvious toll it took on the mind and the body. It started with the drama of divorce and premeditated attack on me. Whether the choices people made were for money, greed, sex, jealousy, hate, or all of the above, these choices were deliberate by all concerned. How many people in your life have been driven off course because of similar madness and stupidity? It meant being thrown into a new world of trauma or for me, "situational anxiety; "all compounded by the Great Recession. Then there was the unexpected setback, the infection that developed from the operation. If I had chosen another hospital, it might have turned out differently, but in the end, it was an act of God for whatever reason. How many people or you yourself have given up and masked the pain, in all forms, with depression or a substance. Large or small, the stage was set.

The reality of street culture: No matter what town, city, commonwealth, state, and country, addiction subcultures exist. Just a handful of years before I lived a life that knew about the subculture's existence but kept it at a distance.

The subculture includes every race, creed, color, nationality, and economic background. My travels covered almost one third of one of the most beautiful, wealthy, and historically important states in the country. I gave you just a taste of the hell that exists. I am just one man alone; I was not a woman, nor did I have a child with me. I was not the unfortunate gay couple that experienced homophobia at the shelter. In short, there are many other real unwanted experiences happening every day.

You must be prepared for stigma: In any plan of recovery from most any addiction, you must prepare for stigma: the emails, the texted messages, the facial expressions, the comments, and many more examples. This communication may be meant to help and support you or it may be intended to hurt you. Of course, there are the people who have the best intentions and strive through their comments to keep you straight; they think they know but they have no clue. You must be in control of your frustration.

Once you have become comfortable with yourself and know the paths that lead to total redemption, stigma may be minimized. Rest assured, stigma can do more damage if not confronted. Comments or actions by others will result in losing friends who once supported you or, worse, deflating what you have and sending you backwards. Talk with your peers and professionals if you need to be prepared.

Health is not a choice: It was not a choice to get a first infection and especially not a choice to get a second infection. It was not a choice to acquire a form of PTSD from blows by a drunken and jealous man. Again, consider others who have fewer health issues and those who have far greater health issues, relatively speaking. No matter what the health issue may be, it can stop our path to a preferred life. It stopped me at least for a time. Yet, I found ways to stop the pain and create a beachhead of hope.

Brian Masters is NOT you: When I started this book, I made it clear that your experience will be different from mine. The events described here led to drinking, loneliness, depression, anxiety, and feelings of desperation. Through positive events, good people, educators, and my belief in a higher power, what seemed to be hopeless changed for the better. I would like to make it clear to you that I know life experiences are different from one person to another. I have shared my background and my stories, so you can understand or identify with my experiences.

What I hope you learn from this book: The take-away is totally up to you. Your perception of my travels, the people I met and the choices I made might be entirely different from mine. By laying out the events I experienced, I can provide insight, which may influence a decision to keep full control of legal substances and stay away from controlled substance. I hope that after reading this book, you will be educated enough to say, "I remember that event or episode from Brian's book! It stops now!"

I cannot say strongly enough that the mental and physical pain you will avoid cannot be put into words. I can touch only on my experience, what I have seen, and my impression of people I met. There are always individuals who have gone through different circumstances, and they could bring a new perspective to the table.

Life's episodes are all open ended: There is no ending to this book. Even if something more permanent happens to my health, events or paths continue to evolve. This means that your path will continue to change, too. However, the action plans and recommended steps are always there for you to execute. The goals and objectives that create hope and acceptable happiness depend on each one of us. They do work, even if the beachhead to sobriety may shrink and fail a first time, second time, or more. It's important to use these tools and keep trying.

The events in this book are real. The people are real. The places are real. The events are real. I often say, "No one would believe what I have been through," or, "Someone needs to let people know what is going on out here, before it happens to them." This book is an attempt to follow through on those thoughts. I want people to recognize what is really happening in institutions, on the streets and in transitional housing. If you can avoid being part of that system, please do just that for yourself and the people you love. If your read the book and understand all three phases, try to reach out and make life better for those in the subculture. You may find yourself creating hope toward a new quality of life for another person.

Epilogue
A Never-Ending Story
The Aftermath

Brian Masters

Even after achieving my goals and regaining a truly better quality of life, I will continue to move forward and have new potential challenges, as would anyone in a similar situation. These challenges could be my health, or my ability to engage in my love of sports, work, or accept the "what is now" versus the "what was then." It is all open ended. Through fate, higher power and determination, I was able to create a beachhead to move forward, focus, and take control. Not long after this book was completed I walked again. I was recruited for a Sales Augmentation project for a $120 million start-up company. I continued my volunteer work for those in need. I continued to repair the damage done in the past ten years, always adding a new set of objectives.

A Check on the People You Met

There are multiple paths. Here are some signs of hope:

•   Len, the gentleman confronted by the young angry man at the Serenity Center, went back to work. He is doing fine and watching his children grow.

•   The St. Vincent DePaul group continues to grow, along with its understanding of the plight of the homeless and addicted.

•   John, who lived with me on Grant Street, moved to a better place and distanced himself from the ongoing drama, a major step in achieving a Beachhead.

- Len got clean with the help of the Center, changing friends, and loving his children.

- The man who hid his bottles took great strides of 90 days, helping him to return to his former, intelligent self.

Is this a tragedy? Is it a cautionary tale? One thing for certain, it is all true.

A Broad Stroke Perspective of My Discoveries

While I was working on this book, the website, part-time and full-time employment and volunteer work, I believe my High Power kept creating a new path. For example, I emailed Dr. William White because I had heard he was an expert on recovery and stigma. We exchanged emails about a few of my posts, including my 11 Action Plan to a "Beachhead" for normalcy.

I came upon Dr. White's work by chance. One of his papers, the Capital Recovery Scale, ranks the conditions of a person's lifestyle in terms of strengths and weakness towards achieving some type of normalcy. The word "capital" refers to assets. The Capital Recovery Scale had a profound impact on me.

I recognized similarities between the Capital Recovery Scale and the 11 Action Plans I described in my blog. These eleven action plans were based on observations of the people and events of my own recovery. I felt they could provide a path of hope for all. This occurred before I knew about Dr. White's Capital Recovery Scale; Dr. White's work validated my own thoughts. Below is a summary of what led me out of my hellhole and into recovery.

The 90-day brain reset started with hospitalization: At the Westborough Transitional Care Facility, I noticed a change in my thinking. Though I could have gone down the street at night or bought someone else's alcohol, I did not. Near the end of November, I no longer thought about drinking. I can explain it as an improved cognitive reasoning about what alcohol would do to me, thereby reducing the impulse to just drink. I remember what the man I called Sam Kenison Ph.D. said at one of his recovery sessions. Yale University did a study that shows an addict needs a minimum of 90 days for the brain to repair. I googled the Yale Study and confirmed its finding. In the summary, the author states, "AA stumbled upon the 90 days of no drinking." I also used the "Reverse Trigger" technique, which means I said or thought of something important to me to immediately dismiss the desire and thoughts of drinking.

Reliable transportation: It was my decision to move back to Marlborough after the nursing home stay. Over the objections of Mike and Martin, I knew that MetroWest Transportation buses would take me where I needed to be. The free PT1 MassHealth ride to preapproved doctor's appointments provided transportation outside the MetroWest bus route.

After working for four and half months on all the Massachusetts RMV requirements to reinstate my license, I was free to buy a car. I bought a Subaru Forester with the SSDI payments. I was free to move on any plan I chose.

The financial plan: Early on I discovered that the best way to avoid misusing your pay or friends' financial help is to have someone else control the checking account; Mike started controlling mine when I was on the streets. When SDDI came into my life and I had accomplished the 90-day brain reset and other steps towards a beachhead to normalcy, I could cognitively reason and control my own finances.

The SSDI payments I received from the federal government were justified to support my health and stability. But what about others, who are not receiving aid? I calculated the financial target a person would have to make to match the SSDI benefits I received. By working forty hours per week, $16 per hour, an individual without dependent children could meet that financial target.

Surrounding myself with the support of friends and family while pushing away from enablers and users; consequently, creating self-motivation and confidence: My separation from enablers and users started when I committed myself. Although the Massachusetts recovery system was flawed in some ways, I decided myself to stay away from the people and locations that would most likely have me saying, "Yes, I will have one." I also discovered the importance of abstaining from sexual relationships while I concentrated on myself. This philosophy of staying away from the opposite sex for a minimum of a year is also an unwritten rule of AA; it helps.

At the same time, I embraced my friendships with Mike and Martin and the phone calls from Jack and Beth, Jim Goodman, Jane and Greg, James and Clare and others. Those phone conversations would come at the times I needed them.

The Serenity Center provided environmental support by allowing me to engage with peers every week. The people there wanted to talk about their problems or have a constructive conversation. The Center created and maintained an environment of support and understanding for all. If a person availed himself of the Center's resources, he could regain a sense of belonging. The Center provided a place and people which could be a spring board to forgiving yourself, understanding others, and achieving goals important to you.

When I moved out of the institutionalized housing phase I ended up on Grant Street. It was not an upscale area and there were users, liquor stores, and constant street dealing. If I chose to leave Grant Street, I would lose the one-year grant; still, that house was not worth the risk. I took the chance and relied on White's character points and my 11 Action Plans to move forward. In doing so, I moved away from any desire to mask the pain with alcohol and participate in the negative drama found only in the subculture.

It could have been my sales and executive training, but having my whiteboard with objectives and daily "to-dos" focused me. Each time I erased a to-do, I knew I had taken one more positive step. It was my tool for self-motivation and planning. I became more self-confident as every item on the list was accomplished. When others tried to stigmatize me, shutting them down became the challenge. I embrace the saying, "I (we) do not have the problem! You have the problem!"

Medical help: I was fortunate to find the right medical help by reaching out for other opinions. By not fully trusting the medical system, I was able to uncover the real cause of my pain. Most people in the medical profession will respect that. If not for Dr. Virginia Dwyer and Mike, I would not have insisted on Gabapentin, which Dr. G immediately agreed to for my neuropathy. The neuropathy was created by the spine operations in 2011 and scar tissue pressing against my right leg nerve canal. The side effect of Gabapentin is the deadening of the pleasure receptor associated with alcohol. This dampened the desire to resume substance use, which would have led to a relapse. This information is based on the work of Dr. Barbara Mason.

For medical solutions to work there must be a trusting relationship between the primary doctor and the patient. Even though I was an individual with addiction issues, using opiates was the only solution for me. By constantly monitoring the drug's effect on my pain and by working with the doctor and staff, I was able to control what could have been another contributor to the disease. Trust and openness must also exist between you and any surgeons you may need. I created my own reporting log to keep track of my medical history. This signaled to the doctors that I was serious and meant business. It also gave me insight into what had happened to me and the consequences. Medical issues are different for each individual and addict, but a positive medical relationship is always a must.

Acknowledgements

- Dr. Virginia Dwyer of Portland, Oregon – without Virginia's hard work, ideas, and encouragement, the book and the website would not exist

- All my family and friends mentioned in Roads to Addiction – Highways to Recovery – they saved my life

- The Jonathan Rizzo Foundation – for funding me in a desperate moment

- Pat B. of Marlborough, MA and SVdP of Marlborough – for Copyediting

- Doctors Ford, Velazquez, and Siric for understanding the true problems and helping me control pain and walk again

- William White for input on Phase 3 and allowing the use of Recovery Capital

- Denise D. for providing important outside perspectives

- The staff of the Serenity Center

- The late June Davis of Marlborough – she took me off the street

- Governor Baker of Massachusetts – for not just talking about the homeless but doing something about the homeless

Sites Shaping the Book's Reality Path

- Wet Brain is diagnosed as a reversible condition:

  http://addictionrealityeducation.com/2015/12/31/there-is-treatme...ndrome-wet-brain/

- Gabapentin's side effect against alcohol: Gabapentin Treatment for Alcohol Dependence. A Randomized Clinical Trial

  https://www.scripps.edu/newsandviews/e_20131111/mason.html

- What an addicted mother can do to her new born:

  http://addictionrealityeducation.com/2016/01/26/destroying-your-...littlest-victims/

Appendix

11 Action Plans to Establish a Beachhead for

Hope and Recovery

While I was homeless I struggled to become sober and regain control of my life. Eventually I came to see homelessness or life in shelters as an opportunity to work with the people at the Serenity Center and research the actions that could provide hope and lead to success. In a strange way, my circumstance allowed me to reflect, document, and analyze how I ended up where I was. By taking this on as serious project with a website and book, I created "Action Plans," which, in any combination, will establish a beachhead to normalcy.

My desire for recovery prompted me to create 11 Action Plans towards a new quality of life; hopefully, these action plans can help you too. As time went on and I acted on specific plans, I stumbled upon tools espoused by other professionals such as AA, SMART RECOVERY, Yale University Medical School, Dr. William White and others. Parts of each came together for the 11 Action Plans. These actions are intended to help create a foundation for eventual recovery. Each plan has its own breakdown of "who, what, where, and when." These are the 11 Action Plans:

• 90 days of mandatory or self-committed institutionalization. This allows the brain to reset itself (see https://www.thefix.com/content/one-big-pain-brain)

• 90 days of classes, meetings, and online recovery websites without _any_ substance use other than doctor prescribed meds.

• Reliable and consistent transportation.

- Support from close friends and family in addition to a sponsor.

- Separate from the town, city, state, friends and family that trigger substance use. Find housing with substance free family, friends, or housing organizations.

- Separate from all those who use, and from inconsistent and/or unsupported paths, until you are confident that your serenity has returned.

- With the support of a physician, experiment with Gabapentin and other medications to block the brain's "use receptors." This may be most important during the 90 commitments; ask your doctor.

- Create and implement a financial support plan, including a budget you can live on. It is best, in the beginning, that you are not in control of the money until you are self-assured the money is not used for substance use.

- Create a personal environment of self-motivation and positive reinforcement. Focus on goals, strategies, and tactics that can be followed every day. Tools such as white board, a calendar and check off lists help.

- Work or volunteer in substance-free organizations or turn to a Higher Power for help and understanding.

- Understand life's "triggers" and learn "reverse trigger" -- thought that neutralize the pain and memories that might keep you trapped in past behaviors.

If you combine any of the above actions that work for you, then you have a chance for a better quality of life going forward. If that happens, this book and the accompanying website (www.addictionrealityeducation.com) Addiction-Reality-Education" will have achieved their goals.

Recovery Capital and Impact on Normalcy

The Recovery Scale and How You Use It

Everyone should ask himself or herself: "Do I want to shake off my present circumstances (disease/addictions) and have a good chance at a positive quality of life?" The following approach will provide a start.

Recovery Capital and using the Recovery Capital Scale by William White and William Cloud: Just like financial capital, the "capital" in Recovery Capital consists of the assets and resources you need to improve your quality of life and achieve normalcy. By giving honest answers to the scale's thirty-five questions, you will discover the strengths and weaknesses of your situation. When you discover the weakness, you can create and implement action plans to correct them, thereby improving your "scale score". This works. See The Capital Recovery Scale Evaluation and Next Steps by William White for detailed information.

http://www.williamwhitepapers.com/pr/Recovery%20Capital%20Scale.pdf

Complementary Increase in Scores: Most people will be happy to learn that improving your score in one category of the scale improves other complementary categories. For example, if your access to transportation improves, scores in the Support and Financial categories will improve because you will be able to travel for a job or make and keep doctors' appointments.

A Technique for Combating Triggers

My experience taught me that certain events, people and circumstances can trigger desires to be where I was before or have what I had before. Whether caused by internal or external stimuli, triggers, in my opinion, are the deadliest ally of self-abuse.

One technique I learned was a "reverse trigger." It is not a long-term solution to stop a craving or urges, but it does quickly destroy or eliminate the memory that triggers the immediate craving or urge. The Reverse Trigger is verbal comment, thought, or physical action/movement that eliminates and replaces the trigger.

My reverse trigger is two words of a widely-said Christian prayer. With those two words, the trigger such as a memory, person, or place is temporarily eliminated. I regain perspective; I am back to reality. Regardless of whether it is a clinically tested technique or just my psyche, it works for me. Hopefully it will work for you.

Recoveryism

In 2006, Tom Horvath, President of SMART Recovery, penned a brief article in which he coined the term Recoveryism. He used the term to depict assertions that a particular approach to addiction recovery was superior to all others – that there really is only ONE effective approach t addiction recovery. Horvath rightly called our attention to a special form of bigotry sometimes exhibited by people who are grateful for their own brand of recovery.

An article by William White gives more information about recoveryism in his article about stigma and recoveryism. http://www.williamwhitepapers.com/blog/2013/08/stigma-and-recoveryism.html

Parts of the Brain and Their Role in

Addiction

In Section 1, I talk about substance use and its effects on the brain. In Section 2, I talk about what I learned from classes about the damaged brain's inability to control reasoning and behavior. As substance use increases and becomes more frequent, the ability of the brain to reason is impaired temporarily or permanently. The two portions of the brain associated with reasoning and behavior are the prefrontal cortex and the limbic system.

The Prefrontal Cortex

The prefrontal cortex (PFC) is the most evolved part of the brain. It occupies the front third of the brain behind the forehead. It is divided into three parts: the dorsal lateral (on the outside surface of the PFC), the inferior orbital, (on the front undersurface of the brain), and the anterior cingulate gyrus, (which runs through the middle of the frontal lobes).

Thought and impulse control are managed by the PFC. The ability to think through the consequences of behavior -- for example, choosing a good mate, interacting appropriately with customers, dealing with difficult children, spending money, driving on the freeway—is essential for success in nearly every aspect of human life. Without proper PFC function, it is difficult to act in consistent, thoughtful ways, and impulses can take over.

The Limbic System

The limbic system refers to the area of the brain that controls emotions and releases the mood regulating hormones and neurotransmitters. Located on both sides of the thalamus beneath the cerebrum, it is responsible for many of our more basic instincts and emotional reactions. For instance, the fight or flight response is governed by the limbic system. The limbic system can be brokayen down into numerous smaller parts. These include:

Thalamus

The thalamus is found at the center of the brain and controls our attention span and our interpretation of pain. It also monitors "input" and helps us to keep track and pay attention to the right sensations in the brain. It likely plays an important role in learning by helping us direct our attention and place importance on the right stimulus, making it more likely that we will retain that information. This explains the phenomenon of the "flashbulb memory," wherein people are likely to remember emotionally charged events in much more vivid detail compared with less emotional events.

Hypothalamus

The hypothalamus controls our mood as well as a range of other bodily sensations such as hunger, thirst, and temperature. It is also responsible for a range of hormonal processes and can thus help to influence the metabolism.

Hippocampus

The hippocampus is also involved in learning and memory, especially for converting short-term memories into long-term memories. If you are asked to remember a phone number while someone gets a pen, then this is your short-term memory at work. When you remember your *own* number permanently and can reproduce it at will, this is an example of using your long-term memory.

The hippocampus is also involved in memories relating to directions and locations.

Housing and Shelters Defined

My experiences led me through institutions, housing, shelters and the street. Here are some definitions:

Permanent: Long-term housing with no maximum length of stay.

Transitional Housing: Time-limited, affordable, supported or independent housing. Tenants can usually remain in transitional housing for up to two or three years.

Emergency Shelter: Short-term shelter for people in crisis. Some emergency shelters also provide meals and support services to the people who stay there.

Shelter or *Dry Housing:* Housing where tenants are not allowed to drink alcohol or use other drugs while in tenancy. Tenants are expected to be "clean" before moving in and actively work on their recovery while living there. Tenants may be discharged from the program if they refuse treatment for a relapse.

Wet Shelter or House: Housing where tenants are not expected to abstain from using alcohol and other drugs, and where entering a rehabilitation program is not a requirement. Tenants have access to recovery services and get to decide if and when to use these services. Wet housing programs follow a harm reduction philosophy.

Damp Housing: Housing where tenants do not need to be "clean" when entering the program but are expected to actively work on recovery from substance use problems.

Low Barrier Housing: Housing where a minimum number of expectations are placed on people who wish to live there. The aim is to have as few barriers as possible to allow more people access to services. In housing, this often means that tenants are not expected to abstain from alcohol or other drugs, or from carrying on with street activities while living on-site, as long as they do not engage in these activities in common areas of the house and are respectful of other tenants and staff.

Private Market: Traditional rental housing that is run by private landlords rather than a housing program.

Subsidized: Housing that receives funding from the government or community organization. Tenants who live in subsidized housing pay rent that is less than market value.

Social Housing: Housing provided by the government (public housing) or a community organization (non-profit housing).

Single Room Occupancy (SRO): Small, one-room apartments that are rented on a monthly or weekly basis. Tenants share common bathrooms and sometimes also share kitchen facilities.

Hardest to House: Refers to people with more complex needs and multiple challenges when it comes to housing, such as mental illness, addiction, other conditions or disabilities, justice-system histories, etc.

Group Home: A home that is shared by many tenants who are generally expected to participate in shared living arrangements and activities. There is usually 24-hour support staff on site.

Spread Sheet of Medical Reports:

A who, what, where, when, medical

specialty,

and actual reports

I have included a copy of the medical spreadsheet I created to track who said what and when. It is extremely important that you request and/or demand the physical MRIs, x-rays and written reports as evidence to back up your work. This task should yield the following:

• Undeniable backup to any confrontation and misunderstanding in the future.

• Valid information for other doctors to work from

• Potentially, increased awareness by medical practitioners that you are serious about your health and well-being.

• Self-motivation and positive reinforcement necessary for normalcy.

Consultation Progression Document

Date:

Primary	Hip		Spine	
Pain Management				
Ford	Siric	Light	Bachi	Beth
Mailer	Good			
	Southern Hospital	UMass Hospital	UMass Hospital	Beth
Hospital	Mass Health	Pain Specialists		

Actual Infection and Complication Report

A Report That Is Hard to Believe

I have included the actual medical report about my infection and its impact on my body and mind. It is hard to believe just reading the facts, so I have included very personal information. Even now, it is hard to believe that I found this document four years after the operations. I found it because I was creating and adding to my medical spreadsheet while piecing together reports for SSDI. Even more amazing is that I asked for any reports from the same rehab center I had gone to in 2011; is it coincidence or a higher power?

Worry If You See or Have these Symptoms

The True Physical Warning Signs of Addiction:

Consider the physical warning signs of addiction as "red flags." Should you consistently notice even a few of these signs in yourself or a loved one, seek help. A good start would be 90 days rehabilitation.

• **The morning headache that will rip your head apart:** Tears come to the eyes because you cannot get to the pain. You need water, a drink, another hit, or meds, but the headache comes back anyway.

• **Eyes:** Your eyes tell it all. Whether you have showered, used extra strength eye drops, or pretend it is an allergy, people will know, especially people who are on the path or have been on the path. Alcohol and heroin are the worst. DO NOT FOOL YOURSELF, PEOPLE WILL KNOW!

• **Overwhelming thirst for fluids:** The body is gravely dehydrated, so much that the stomach contracts with pain. Combined with the swelled brain and body shakes, dehydration can lead to seizures and shock.

• **Pale face:** No matter what color your skin at birth, you will have a pale face. You will wear it every day that you are an active addict.

• **Shakes:** Different parts of the body will shake uncontrollably. You will not be able to stop or control the shakes. Every task becomes an effort; handing over money, typing, holding a bottle without spilling, starting a car, holding a tool, etc. AND DO NOT FOOL YOURSELF--everyone knows.

- **Sweats:** Any moisture in the body comes out through your pores. Noticeably, it comes through the face and hands. Your underarm smell becomes unbearable. EVERYONE CAN SEE IT AND SMELL IT!

- **Smell of your body**: Your body develops a distinctive smell that radiates from your pores. It could be the heroin, vodka/beer/whiskey, or methadone. Your clothes and sheets absorb the stench. EVERYONE CAN SMELL WHAT IT IS--THERE IS NO HIDING IT. I'm not the first person to notice this. Listen to Lynard Skynard's song "That Smell" and read the lyrics. This is what I'm talking about.

- **Inability to walk, work, and endure sports:** Even when sober, your ability to walk or talk is damaged. Agility is eliminated to the point you puke.

- **Blackouts:** You cannot remember what you did, what you said, and who you met for a period. Blackouts are a major warning signal that you need help. See my blog post on Blackouts: Death, Jail or Life (https://addictionrealityeducation.com/2015/11/21/blackouts-the-choice-is-life-death-or-jail/)

- **No control of shitting and/or pissing:** Your bladder will give you NO warning. If there is just a little urge to go, you better run for the bathroom or stop the car. Your urine will come and wet the clothes and there is no stopping it! Your bowel movement will become very soft. Without notice, the body will decide to let it go. The watery crap will spread either down the leg and/or spread sideways over your clothes and ass. AGAIN, there is no hiding the wet and brown stains on your body. For good measure, the smell is more toxic than usual. EVERYONE KNOWS!

- **Snorting at night and puking in the morning:** The sound is very distinctive. Anyone in the house or outside the door know what is going down. Later in the day or in the morning, the fun wears off. Now comes the incredible pain to the head and nerves. Withdrawals. Now you beg for more or pay for pain killers to stop the torture in the body. THERE IS NO STOPPING IT!

• **Uncontrollable vomiting:** Normally in the morning, your stomach contracts and you are FORCED to get sick, loud and clear. If you are lucky, it happens only once but usually it lasts for three or five rounds. It can happen anywhere and at any time. And it smells. YOU CAN NOT HIDE IT!

• **Seizures:** You are off to the hospital. For those of us who use drugs, particularly those of us who binge or use to excess, seizures can occur. Sometimes they happen just before or as someone is overdosing or when withdrawing from a drug (e.g., benzos, alcohol). Seizures are the body's rather intense way of telling us that we have been pushing our bodies too hard for too long. Drug Induced Seizure (see https://blackpoppymag.wordpress.com/the-a-z-of-overdose/drug-induced-seizures/)

• **Hallucinations:** You start seeing or interacting with something or someone that does not exist. It may seem very real but when you check outcomes from the event, they do not exist. According to Google substance abuse is a common cause of hallucinations.

Made in the USA
Middletown, DE
14 June 2018